IMMEASURABLE

REFLECTIONS ON THE SOUL OF MINISTRY IN THE AGE OF CHURCH, INC.

SKYE JETHANI

MOODY PUBLISHERS

CHICAGO

Portions of chapter 18 are adapted from *The Divine Commodity* by Skye Jethani. Copyright © 2009 by Skye Jethani. Used by permission of Zondervan. www.zondervan.com.

Unless otherwise noted, Scripture quotations are from the ESV® Bible (The Holy Bible, English Standard Version®), copyright © 2001 by Crossway, a publishing ministry of Good News Publishers. Used by permission. All rights reserved.

Some names and details have been changed to protect the privacy of individuals.

Edited by Matthew Boffey
Interior Design: Erik M. Peterson
Cover Design: Faceout Studio
Cover image of penrose triangle copyright © 2017 by Vector FX / Shutterstock (278280464). All rights reserved.

Library of Congress Cataloging-in-Publication Data

Names: Jethani, Skye, 1976- author.
Title: Immeasurable : reflections on the soul of ministry in the Age of
   Church, Inc. / Skye Jethani.
Description: Chicago : Moody Publishers, 2017.
Identifiers: LCCN 2017029077 (print) | LCCN 2017035702 (ebook) | ISBN
   9780802496218 | ISBN 9780802416193
Subjects: LCSH: Pastoral theology. | Church work. | Fame--Religious
   aspects--Christianity. | Clergy--Public opinion.
Classification: LCC BV4011.3 (ebook) | LCC BV4011.3 .J48 2017 (print) |
DDC
   253--dc23
LC record available at https://lccn.loc.gov/2017029077

ISBN: 978-0-8024-1619-3

We hope you enjoy this book from Moody Publishers. Our goal is to provide high-quality, thought-provoking books and products that connect truth to your real needs and challenges. For more information on other books and products written and produced from a biblical perspective, go to www.moodypublishers. com or write to:

Moody Publishers
820 N. LaSalle Boulevard
Chicago, IL 60610

1 3 5 7 9 10 8 6 4 2

Printed in the United States of America

Dedicated to:

Henri Nouwen
Brennan Manning
Dallas Willard
Eugene Peterson

"There were giants in the earth in those days."[1]

CONTENTS

"There are no measures which can set forth
the immeasurable greatness of Jehovah. . . . If we
cannot measure we can marvel."
— C. H. SPURGEON

INTRODUCTION

ALL PREACHERS should be grateful for time limits. Without them every sermon would eventually drift into contradiction or outright heresy. This tendency was on full display at a gathering of pastors I attended about ten years ago. The preacher that night was a riveting orator, easily capable of keeping the audience engaged for hours, not merely minutes. He deployed this skill to regale us with a 24-point sermon. (I'm not exaggerating.)

One of his early points emphasized the Holy Spirit's unpredictable and sovereign nature. "The wind blows where it wishes," Jesus said to Nicodemus. "You hear its sound, but you do not know where it comes from or where it goes. So it is with everyone who is born of the Spirit" (John 3:8).

Later in the sermon, somewhere between points 16 and 22, the preacher used a very different analogy. "When the gospel is preached," he declared, with his hands animating the metaphor, "it is like fighter jets flying in a tight formation. The preacher is the lead F-18, turning and diving and climbing. And right on his wing, following every move, is the Holy Spirit." In the same sermon, within less than an hour, the Spirit had been demoted from an unpredictable whirlwind to the preacher's ever-predictable wingman.

The sermon illustrated more than the time-tested wisdom of sticking to just three points. It also revealed the magnetic pull of modern ministers toward control and away from mystery. In our enlightened age of metadata and best practices, we believe that ministry—like everything else—can be accomplished through proven principles of control.

I call this sub-spiritual, mechanical approach to ministry "Church, Inc." It is shorthand for ministry devoid of mystery, for pastors who assume that the exercise of their calling is a matter of skill more than the gravity of their soul. It represents the exchange of the transcendent calling of Christian ministry with mere management of religious institutions and services. If ministry is encountering the heat and light of an uncontrollable sun, Church, Inc. is the tanning salon in the local strip mall.

The attraction of Church, Inc. to religious consumers is easy enough to grasp, but how do we explain its appeal to ministers? It would be easy to blame the popularity of Church, Inc. on the influence of business principles among pastors, but that fails to identify the root cause. To be fair, the church has always adopted the dominant forms and structures of the culture surrounding it. Richard Halverson, the former chaplain of the United States Senate, observed:

> In the beginning the church was a fellowship of men and women centered on the living Christ. Then the church moved to Greece, where it became a philosophy. Then it moved to Rome, where it became an institution. Next, it moved to Europe, where it became a culture. And, finally, it moved to America, where it became an enterprise.[1]

Many of us in ministry are drawn to the strategies tested and proven by leaders of secular corporations because they are the most celebrated and successful leaders in our culture. Just as the Greeks exalted philosophers and the Romans exalted soldiers, we exalt entrepreneurs and CEOs. Our culture celebrates their accomplishments and seeks to emulate their strategies.

But is that the only reason we are drawn to Church, Inc.?

Adam and Eve were not merely tempted because the fruit was "a delight to the eyes," but because of the serpent's promise that it would make them "like God." Likewise, the allure of Church, Inc. is not merely its offer of a better, more effective approach to ministry. It's in its promise to make us like God. Simply put, it tempts us with control. In Church, Inc. we occupy the lead F-18 and the Spirit follows our lead. The outcomes remain safely in our hands rather than His.

This desire for measurable, controllable outcomes in ministry, whether rooted in the values of our culture or the rebellion of our souls, betrays the essence of our faith. All of the inexorable doctrines of Christianity are immeasurable, sometimes paradoxical, mysteries. Has anyone fully grasped the eternal union of God as three persons? Who has delineated the nature of Jesus as both fully God and fully man? After two millennia we still argue about the interplay of human will and divine sovereignty, and fellowships are bonded and broken over our feeble attempts to explain what exactly did or did not happen on that old rugged cross.

If salvation, humanity, and God Himself are enveloped in impenetrable mystery, why do we assume ministry—which stands at the intersection of all three—to be a calculable science? Why are we unwilling to surrender to the immeasurability of our calling and discover a beauty and value beyond the empty promises of Church, Inc.?

That is the central question animating each chapter of this book. What follows is a collection of essays, letters, articles, and reflections about the challenges of ministry in our age of industrial discipleship. Each is intended to draw ministers toward deeper reflections about their calling, the condition of their soul, and the meaning of their work. Each essay concludes with questions to jump-start such reflection and begin the process of application. The chapters are thematically arranged, but they do not need to be read in sequence. Instead, I encourage you to engage the timely topics and return to others as needed.

There are countless ministry books to help you answer the question, "How . . . ?" They focus on the skills necessary to manage a church or fulfill a ministry task, and every minister needs such books within their library. But this book is not one of them. I hope you find some helpful and practical advice in these pages, but I feel that in the mechanical ministry culture we occupy, we need to step back and reconsider what ministry is, what is unique about our calling, and how it remains beyond the scope of mere leadership principles and best practices. I've written this book to challenge assumptions and provoke new ideas about what faithfulness in the age of Church, Inc. can look like.

To do that, we must deconstruct some of the practices and values you may have uncritically assimilated into your vision of ministry and your identity as a pastor. That deconstruction won't be comfortable. It never is. With these falsehoods uprooted and tossed aside, however, there will be new space for a more life-giving vision of your calling to germinate. My hope is that as you rediscover the immeasurability of ministry, you will marvel anew at the work to which you've been called—and at the One who has called you to it.

AMBITION

1

WHEN I ENTERED SEMINARY, I was humbled by many of my classmates. While we all suffered through "suicide Greek" (an intense six-week summer course that only a gifted linguist with a penchant for self-flagellation would enjoy), I learned that some students sacrificed far more than others to pursue a call into pastoral ministry.

Scott left his position as a Navy pilot with a stable salary and excellent benefits. David left his management job with an automaker and relocated his family. He attended classes all day and studied while working as a night security guard. I have no idea when he slept.

Gregory, an engineer from China, brought his wife and two young girls from Hong Kong to Chicago—he'd never seen snow before, let alone twelve inches of it covering his car. In six months Gregory taught himself enough English to successfully translate the New Testament from Greek into English, and then into Cantonese for his congregation in Chicago's Chinatown.

These pastors represent the power of godly ambition. Their desire to serve God and people was the engine that drove them to make enormous sacrifices.

But seminary revealed the dark side of ambition as well. On my first day in a small class, when asked to introduce ourselves and say why we had entered seminary, the first student said, "I'm here because I'm going to be the next Bill Hybels." (Hybels is a popular megachurch pastor.) Really, I thought. Someone should tell him that Bill Hybels isn't dead. I don't think we need another one yet.

The next said, "My grandfather was a pastor, my father was a pastor, and I'm supposed to be a pastor, too." Someone call a counselor. This one has daddy issues.

The third student revealed his three-year plan to become senior pastor and then transform his congregation into a megachurch. "My denomination wants me to have an MDiv degree," he said, "but once they see I can grow a big church, I don't think they'll make me finish the program." An ego the size of Donald Trump's. Good grief, I thought.

As the introductions continued around the room, a frightening realization entered my mind: What if my motivations for being here are just as questionable? Seminary had introduced me to remarkable women and men with godly devotion and drive, but it also showed me the shadow side of pastoral ambition. It can drive us to make great sacrifices in service to God and others, or it can be a veneer that hides far less noble motivations. What appears to be love or devotion externally may actually be fueled by profound insecurity or even, in rare cases, pathological mental illness.

Even those with a healthy motivation sometimes need our ambition engines tuned up, a realignment toward Christ and away from self-centered desires. Discerning when we require an overhaul is the dilemma. There is no "check engine" light on the dashboard of our soul. But Scripture does offer wisdom in recognizing when our ambitions are misfiring.

Old Testament figures like Moses and Jeremiah were reluctant leaders. They did not want power or influence and at times actively resisted God's call into leadership. There is something noble about a reluctant leader, a sense that we can trust them with power because they don't want it. Perhaps that is why we create so many fictional heroes with this quality. Batman, Harry Potter, Katniss Everdeen—they all become leaders out of circumstance and necessity rather than desire for acclaim. It is the opposite of what we so often see in others and suspect about ourselves.

Moses and Jeremiah were this way. God put a "fire in their bones" that they could not extinguish. They were compelled to lead and speak, seemingly against their will. They remind us that the call to leadership is a result of God's grace; it doesn't come from our desire for acclaim. But is humble reluctance what we should expect in every godly leader?

Not according to the New Testament. Peter says that elders ought to lead willingly and not under compulsion (1 Peter 5:2), and Paul affirms those who aspire to leadership

(1 Tim. 3:1). We should remember, however, that while being a church leader in the first century may have offered a person more honor within the Christian community, it also often carried the likelihood of greater persecution by those outside of it. In other words, leadership carried a cost.

Still, the affirmation of willing leaders with a desire to teach and guide God's people is evidence that ambition is not inherently bad. When it is sparked by our communion with Christ, it can be a righteous energy that drives us toward the work of God. It can inspire us to take risks, try new approaches, or venture to new lands. The challenge, therefore, is to recognize the volatile and combustible nature of ambition. When paired with godliness and humility, and guided by a love for others, it can ignite life-giving change in the world. Where would we be without the ambitions of William Wilberforce, Martin Luther King Jr., or Dorothy Day?

Ambition, when combined with the accelerants of ego and insecurity, can become a source of great destruction.

But any fuel that can accomplish so much good carries inherent dangers as well. Ambition, when combined with the accelerants of ego and insecurity, can become a source of great destruction. The drive to achieve can backfire on a leader, causing terrible harm to families, congregations, and the work of God in the world.

You know the pattern. A young Christian with strong communication abilities discovers that others are drawn to him. Conflating the affirmation of an audience with a calling from God, the young man decides to start a church. He genuinely wants to see others engage with God, but there is another motive lurking beneath the surface. The church grows quickly. He soon finds himself in the company of other high-octane church leaders with even larger, more influential ministries. Comparing himself to them makes his ambition burn even hotter. Next come books, conferences, and media appearances. The inner apparatus of the church shifts subtly from growing disciples to growing the pastor's platform. Just as he reaches the pinnacle of influence—everything implodes.

Sadly such stories are all too common. The problem was not a flawed church structure (they are all flawed) or even the ambition of the church leader (we are all ambitious). The problem was what fueled the ambition. Rather than the life-giving fire of communion with Christ, he chose the explosive power of an insecure ego.

As I learned in seminary, we are all a mix of godly and ungodly ambitions. In His power and wisdom, our Lord can use even those driven by selfish motives (Phil. 1:15–18), but we certainly don't want to be counted among them.

REFLECTION AND APPLICATION

When did you first sense a draw toward ministry? Looking back, can you identify both healthy and unhealthy motives in your decision?

What are the warning signs—the lights on your soul's dashboard—that your ambition is being fueled by ungodly desires? Who recognizes these warning lights when you do not?

EFFECTIVENESS

2

COMPARE TWO LEADERS. Leader A lifted an entire nation in a time of despair. He mobilized his people against unimaginable odds with a clear vision and inspiring passion. He launched a movement that has impacted literally everyone alive today. He set in motion an industrial and scientific revolution that produced the first computer, the first jet airplane, began human exploration of space, and unlocked the mystery of nuclear energy. Almost every aspect of the modern world has, in one way or another, been influenced by this man. By the time he died at the age of only fifty-six, everyone on the planet knew his name. Without a doubt, Leader A changed the world.

Leader B lived during the same era. In fact, he died just twenty-one days before Leader A, but his life was very different. At the height of his influence, Leader B ran a school with just a hundred students. He wrote a few books but was not widely regarded. He was beloved by his friends and family and had a reputation for being both intelligent and faithful, but at the time of his death almost no one knew his name, and most considered his life's work unfulfilled—including Leader B himself.

So, given the choice, which leader's strategies would you rather study? Which man's life would you rather emulate? Which leadership conference would you rather attend—the one featuring a keynote address by Leader A, or the one with a small workshop in a back hall facilitated by Leader B? If you are inspired by the world-changing effectiveness of Leader A, congratulations! You've chosen Adolf Hitler. Leader B was Dietrich Bonhoeffer, the German pastor who was executed by the Nazis for his relentless opposition to Hitler.

My point is simple: effectiveness isn't everything. And yet, we remain enamored with it. A few years ago, a prominent Christian leader speaking to sixty thousand young people said, "The only thing I am afraid of is living an insignificant life." Many of us can relate to that fear. The problem, however, is how we've been shaped by the culture—both inside and outside the church—to define significance. Everywhere we go, we are bombarded with the message that our significance is proportional to how much we change the world. Those few who actually become "world changers" are rewarded with the eternal life of Christian celebrity. The rest of us, however, are condemned to the second death of obscurity.

From where did this idea come that we're all supposed

to change the world? Searching book titles in the Harvard University library database reveals something surprising. In the last fifteen years, five times as many books with phrases like "change the world" in the title have been published than in the entire twentieth century. It seems that Millennials, more than any previous generation, have been shaped by a culture that equates effectiveness with significance.

When this idea is carried into the Christian faith, we come to believe that our value to *God* is rooted in how much we achieve for Christ and His kingdom. We may say we are doing it all for the glory of God and for the mission of the gospel, but often there is a deeper motive, a shadow mission to prove our significance through our effectiveness. I call it the Idol of Effectiveness, and I saw it on display years ago with a group of college students I mentored.

There were about ten of us gathered one night, and the students wanted to talk about their ongoing struggles with sinful habits. I asked each student to answer this question: In the midst of your sin, how do you think God views you?

The first student was a missionary kid. Decades before, she said, her parents had been students at a Christian college when a revival occurred. They committed themselves to overseas missions. The young woman shared about growing up in a wonderful family, with parents committed to God's work, and in a fantastic Christian community. "Now I'm at a Christian college," she said, "and how is God ever going to use me the way He's used my parents if I'm still struggling with sin?"

The next student quoted Scripture. He said, "To whom

much is given much is expected. God has given me so much, and I think He's disappointed with my sin. He expects more from me."

One after another they shared a similar sentiment, sometimes fighting back tears. They spoke of God's disappointment and of their fear that they won't be effective for Him in the world. Finally, after everyone shared, it got back to me, and I asked them a few more questions. "How many of you grew up in Christian homes?" They all raised their hands. "How many of you grew up in churches where the gospel was preached?" Again, they all raised their hands.

"What's so tragic," I said to them, "is that after twenty years in the church and now attending an evangelical college, not one of you gave the right answer. It didn't occur to any of you to say that in the midst of your sin God loves you."

Those young people had absorbed the idolatry of the evangelical movement. It is in the air we breathe. It is the water we swim in. We have replaced the love of the living God with sacrifices to the Idol of Effectiveness. When we bow to this idol, it steals our joy and replaces it with an unbearable burden. We begin to see everything—our value, our identity, even the absence or presence of sin in our lives—through the lens of effectiveness. But the most tragic lie the Idol of Effectiveness tells us is that a life spent in service for God is the same as a life with God.

I believe the most frightening passage in the Bible is in Matthew 7. There Jesus says that on the Day of Judgment many will come to him saying, "Lord, Lord, did we not prophecy in your name, and cast out demons in your name, and do many mighty works in your name?" But Jesus will say to them, "I never knew you; depart from me." These are people who are absolutely convinced that they belong to Christ because they have spent their lives on mission for Him, and they have been very effective. They have preached in His name, they have fought evil in His name, and they have performed miracles in His name. And yet, they never knew Him. That is the great danger of confusing effectiveness for God as intimacy with God. For me the most frightening word in this most frightening passage is "many." Jesus says *many* will come to Him on that day completely convinced that they belong to Him because of their effectiveness.

You may be thinking, *How is that possible? How can they do those amazing things and not know Christ? How can they be so effective in ministry and be rejected at the judgment?* The Idol of Effectiveness has power because it causes us to look at the wrong fruit. We become enamored by relevance, power, impact, and how much we have changed the world. While all of those things are measures of effectiveness, none of them are a measure of faithfulness.

In Numbers 20, Moses has just led the people of God out of Egypt and into the wilderness. There they begin to complain about not having any water. They're ready to riot against Moses. So he falls on his face before the Lord in the tabernacle and prays for a solution. God says to him, "Speak to the rock and it will bring forth water for the people and their animals" (see Num. 20:8).

Something happened to Moses after leaving the presence of God, however, and rather than speaking to the rock as he had been commanded, Moses struck it twice with his staff. Incredibly, a miracle happened anyway. Water flowed abundantly. The people were saved. Moses was a hero.

Now consider the scene from a human point of view, or from the perspective of the Idol of Effectiveness. Was Moses's ministry effective? Absolutely! By any human standard, Moses was an effective leader. Was his ministry powerful? Yes, a miracle occurred! Was Moses's ministry relevant? Clearly. It's difficult to be more relevant than giving water to thirsty people in a desert. Was his ministry strategic? Without a doubt. He equipped the people with what they needed to reach their goal, the Promised Land. If Moses were here today, he'd be selling books on 3 Steps to Drawing Water from Rocks. He'd be speaking on the ministry conference circuit and hosting webinars for dehydrated churches. From a human perspective, Moses was outrageously effective.

But what about from the Lord's perspective? Not so much. God was far less impressed. In fact, Moses was punished severely for his disobedience. He was forbidden from entering the Promised Land. Instead, the Lord determined he would die within sight of it. Why? Because God does not judge our effectiveness. He judges our faithfulness. It's clear in Numbers 20 that God decided to perform a miracle in spite of Moses, not because of him.

So, when we focus on effectiveness, we are focusing on the wrong fruit. We assume that if people are coming to faith, if the church is growing, if the world is changing, then we must be right with God. But in fact God may be working in spite of us, not because of us. And here's the real truth we don't like to admit—every time God works, it is in spite of us. He does not need us to accomplish His work. If He did, He wouldn't be a God worthy of our worship. There is an important truth that ministers need to hear as much as, if not more than, everyone else: *God does not need you. He wants you.* He did not send His Son to recruit you to change the world. He sent His Son to reconcile you to Himself. Your value to God is not in your effectiveness, but in your presence.

> Before we are called to something or somewhere, our highest calling is to Someone.

I'm not saying the mission of Christ isn't important. I'm saying it's not most important. Tim Keller has reminded us that an idol is a good thing that we make into an ultimate thing. Effectiveness is a good thing, but it's not the ultimate thing. I care about the mission of God too much to care about the mission of God too much.

If we are to slay the Idol of Effectiveness, we must look for the right fruit both in ourselves and in the leaders we choose to follow. That fruit is not relevance or power or global impact. The fruit of a life lived in communion with Jesus Christ is love, joy, peace, patience, kindness, gentleness, goodness, faithfulness, and self-control. If we are to slay the Idol of Effectiveness then we must recapture the glorious truth that before we are called to something or somewhere, our highest calling is to Someone.

What "fruit" does your ministry measure? How might this make you susceptible to the Idol of Effectiveness? Reflect on a season when your ministry was effective, but your soul was unhealthy. What questions can you regularly ask as leaders to ensure you see more than the human perspective of your ministry?

Ask your leaders if they are experiencing joy. If so, where? How? If not, what is stealing it from them? If those at the center of your ministry are not experiencing the fruit of the Spirit, why would you expect those at the periphery to? Use this to begin a longer conversation about the fruit of the Spirit in your community.

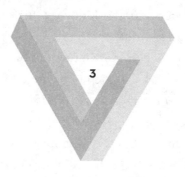

WASTEFULNESS

EFFECTIVE. EFFICIENT. PRACTICAL. It is remarkable how often one hears these words in the world of Church, Inc. Their frequency may reflect our desire to be wise stewards of the resources God has entrusted to us, or they may reflect the influence of a culture that strives for control and values ROI (return on investment) above all else. I suspect both motivations are at play.

Scripture rightly warns us to be careful with money. It is a tempting master broadcasting a siren promise of omnipotence—the power to control one's life and circumstances. We have all heard the heartbreaking stories of pastors lured into wealth's maelstrom. We have also heard the stories of ministries that simply mismanaged their finances and slowly, quietly disappeared beneath a tide of debt. Regularly telling these tales of woe keeps church leaders vigilant. They provoke us to be effective, efficient, and practical. But might these values carry a hidden danger, perhaps even more perilous than wealth?

When efficiency becomes an unquestioned value within Church, Inc., we risk embracing the ungodly ethic of utilitarianism. Rather than seeing people as inherently valuable regardless of their usefulness, we begin to wonder how we might extract more money, volunteer energy, missional output, or influence from them. Our goal as pastors shifts from serving and equipping to extracting and using. Rather than asking how we might love someone, we wonder how we might leverage them, and we can hide these ungodly motivations from others (and even from ourselves) by appealing to the universally celebrated virtue of stewardship. After all, isn't it poor stewardship to have a CEO sitting in the pews every week and not utilize his wealth and leadership capacity for the church? And would a good steward invest the church's resources into young adults who are too transient to become leaders and too poor to give back?

We condemn our culture for devaluing human life it deems useless—the unborn, the elderly, the mentally disabled, the immigrant, the poor, etc.—yet the same utilitarian values of efficiency and practicality that fuel these societal sins are no less common within the church. As ministers of the gospel of Christ, we must stand boldly against the popular belief that everything and everyone exists to be useful. We must remember that in His grace God has created some things not to be used, but simply to behold. After all, the Lord not only created a garden for the man and woman with every tree that was useful for food, but also every tree that was beautiful to the eye (Gen. 2:9). Sometimes we are the most like God when we are being the most impractical.

The graceful, "wasteful" nature of God was revealed shortly before Jesus' death. While reclining at a table, a woman poured a very expensive flask of oil upon His feet. When His disciples saw this, they were appalled. Like many church leaders today, they could only see through the lens of practicality. "This ointment could have been sold for more than three hundred denarii and given to the poor," said Judas, and the disciples rebuked the woman.

"Leave her alone," Jesus shot back. "Why do you trouble her? She has done a beautiful thing to me."

For those who believe that the beautiful must submit to the practical, it is impossible to view the woman's action as anything but wasteful. The disciples saw the spilled oil as a lost opportunity. To them the oil was only a commodity to be utilized and exchanged for a measurable outcome. What they interpreted as a waste, however, Jesus saw as priceless. He recognized the spilled oil as beautiful, impractical worship. True worship can never be wasteful because it seeks no return on investment. True worship is never a transaction. It is always a gift—an extravagant, "wasteful" gift.

True worship can never be wasteful because it seeks no return on investment.

Perhaps our captivity to efficiency, like that of the disciples, explains the dismissive posture many pastors have toward the arts. Sure, we appreciate beautiful architecture, music, and paintings if they serve the practical goal of communicating a biblical truth or drawing people through the church's doors. But art for art's sake? How could that possibly glorify Christ? Why would that be a wise investment?

Artists who cultivate beauty in the world remind us that the most precious things are often the least useful. Artists provoke us to see the world differently—not simply as a bundle of resources to be used, but as a gift to be received. Therefore, the creative arts serve as a model of God's grace, and how the church affirms and celebrates the vocations of artists is likely to inform its vision of God. As Andy Crouch said, "If we have a utilitarian attitude toward art, if we require it to justify itself in terms of its usefulness to our ends, it is very likely that we will end up with the same attitude toward worship, and ultimately toward God."[1]

To combat the utilitarianism of our culture, and to foster a right vision of God, perhaps the church needs to learn to be more wasteful rather than less. Maybe there is a time for the voices of practicality to remain silent as the artists prophetically call us back to extravagant worship, to behold God rather than to use Him. And maybe it is good to embrace the impracticality of having young children, the mentally handicapped, and other "useless" people in our worship gatherings as a way of valuing what the world discards, detoxifying such ungodly values from our own souls.

And perhaps the church should spend money on what the world deems impractical and wasteful. When the voices of the world cry out in protest against the church, as they inevitably will, maybe the voice of Jesus will speak in defense of His precious, often useless bride: "Why do you trouble her? She has done a beautiful thing to me."

REFLECTION AND APPLICATION

Efficiency is good, but how has your ministry become enslaved by it? How has it become an idol that has blinded you to the value of inefficient and impractical things?

Read Psalm 27 and consider the impracticality of David's desire. What has captured his heart, and how does he respond? Use this psalm to guide your own prayers.

VAMPIRES

IN 1998, author Anne Rice shocked her readers and the publishing world when she announced she would never write another vampire book. She authored the bestselling Vampire Chronicles series, including *Interview with a Vampire,* which some folks credit with launching the whole vampire (and now zombie) obsession seen in popular culture. But in '98 Rice said she would never write those kinds of books again—ever.

Why? Because that year she committed her life to Christ. She said, "My life is commmitted to Christ the Lord. My books will be a reflection of that commitment." Her fans pushed back, begging her to keep writing about vampires, witches, and ghosts. Rice said, "Is Christ our Lord not the ultimate supernatural hero, the ultimate outsider, the ultimate immortal of them all?"[1]

Instead she went on to write two novelizations of the life

of Jesus based on the gospel of Luke (which are absolutely brilliant books, by the way). But then in 2010, twelve years after her first shocking announcement, she made another. From Anne Rice's Facebook page:

> Today I quit being a Christian. I'm out. I remain committed to Christ as always but not to being "Christian" or to being part of Christianity. . . . In the name of Christ, I refuse to be anti-gay. I refuse to be anti-feminist. I refuse to be anti-artificial birth control. I refuse to be anti-Democrat. I refuse to be anti-secular humanism. I refuse to be anti-science. I refuse to be anti-life. In the name of Christ, I quit Christianity and being Christian. Amen.

Her post triggered a frenzy on social media with thousands of people reposting and "liking" her statement.

Rice identified many of her objections: the perception that Christianity is anti-gay or anti-woman, too affiliated with politics, too exclusionary, etc. But what caught my attention was the distinction Rice made between her ongoing commitment to Christ and her disillusionment with Christianity.

Real moral issues aside, Anne Rice's journey represents what more and more people are reporting. They are drawn to Christ, they want to follow Him as Lord, but they are finished with this aspect of Church, Inc. Whether, like Rice, they are done pledging allegiance to cultural/political Christianity, or are simply exhausted by the burdens laid on them by church leaders, there is a desire to abandon the institutional structures of Church, Inc. To a growing number of people, the church feels like a vampire sucking the life out of them.

Dozens of books have been published to dicipher this trend over the last few years, and I don't think there is a single, simple answer. To complicate the matter even more, it isn't just young adults who are dropping out of church. Older folks are, too. People like Anne Rice, who have spent decades engaged in—and sometimes leading—the church, are now leaving it. In fact, one extensive study by Josh Packard found that the people most committed to Christ were the most likely to quit church.[2]

A few years ago, I traveled all over the country working on a project called "This Is Our City," profiling the stories of Christians who see their vocations in business, government, the arts, education, entertainment, and science as part of God's work in the world. I met some deeply devoted and remarkable people, but what struck me was how few of them were deeply connected to a local church. They were committed to Christ and actively serving Him in the world, but when asked about their church, most just shrugged their shoulders. Among those who *did* attend a church regularly, I found that, for the most part, their church did not factor into their calling in any meaningful way.

That disconnect is what worries me. Rather than tackle the larger issue of people leaving the faith, I want to know why people who are committed to Christ are leaving the church. Why do they see Christ as giving them life but view the church as taking it from them?

The Anti-Institutional Culture

First, we must define what we mean by *church*. In the English language, we use the word in four ways. First, we use it when referring to a *building* used for Christian worship. "Did you see the new church being built over on Main Street?" Second, we use church when referring to a Christian worship *event*. When we say, "Do you go to church on Sunday?" we're asking if you worship or attend a religious service. Third, we use the word church when talking about an *institution* with officers, employees, programs, and resources pursuing Christian goals. "I made a donation to the church." That means I gave my money to a 501(c)(3) nonprofit organization to fund its buildings, programs, staff, etc. Fourth, church can mean a *community* of women, men, and children who belong to Christ and live under His reign—as in, "Bill is part of my church." He's part of my local assembly of Christians.

While all of these definitions are commonly used in English, only one of them is commonly used in the New Testament—the fourth. That's where the problem begins. Most of us know, biblically speaking, that the church is not a building or simply an event. Things get more muddled, however, when we move into the third and fourth definitions. When you say "church," do you have in mind the organization, leaders, budgets, and programs? Or do you imagine your community of Christian sisters and brothers?

It is important to acknowledge this ambiguity because it plays a big part in understanding why people are leaving the church. When I ask more probing questions of the church dropouts I've met, what I discover is that most are not rejecting Christian community or the fellowship of sisters and brothers committed to Jesus Christ. Instead they are rejecting further involvement with a church institution. They aren't rejecting the New Testament's definition of church, but the 501(c)(3) nonprofit organizations commonly called "churches."

This distinction has been confirmed by research. In the 1970s, Gallup found that 68 percent of Americans had strong or high confidence in the institutional church. In fact, churches outranked all other institutions as the most respected institutions in America. Today, confidence in the church has declined to 42 percent, and among younger Americans it's even lower.[3] Commitment to an institutional church simply isn't as important to Americans anymore, but that doesn't mean people aren't committed to Christian community.

Before you become too discouraged, this decline must be seen in a larger context. Gallup has found that over the last forty years, Americans have lost confidence in virtually all of our culture's institutions. This distrust is most evident among the young.[4] My generation (Generation X) and Millennials (those born after 1980) have a strong aversion to institutions, and the bigger the institutions, the more distrustful we are.

That's a fascinating inversion from earlier generations, who believed that big institutions were stable, secure, and therefore worthy of trust. For example, Baby Boomers were attracted to big churches. They're the generation that

invented the modern megachurch. That made sense, because for Boomers large meant legitimate. *If a church is big,*
they reasoned, *it must be doing something right.*

That logic is foreign to me and my peers. We've been
shaped by a culture where institutions fail, governments
lie, churches hide their scandals, and even the most sacred
and intimate institution, marriage, was shaken when our
fathers walked out the door with a hastily packed suit-
case. We now occupy a post-Watergate, post-marriage,
post-Enron, post-Lehman Brothers, post-Snowden world.
For younger Americans, big doesn't mean legitimate; big
means corrupt.

In 2012, *The Atlantic* ran a thoughtful article on this
trend called, "How Americans Lost Trust in Our Greatest
Institutions." The subtitle captured the trend: "It's not just
Washington. Across the country, citizens' faith in their city
halls, newspapers, and churches is fading." As a generation,
the research shows, we just aren't willing to commit ourselves to institutions anymore. Laura Hansen, a sociologist
cited in the article, put it this way:

> We lost [faith] in the media: Remember Walter
> Cronkite? We lost it in our culture: You can't point
> to a movie star who might inspire us, because we
> know too much about them. We lost it in politics,
> because we know too much about politicians' lives.
> We've lost it—that basic sense of trust and confi-
> dence—in everything.[5]

But this loss of confidence in institutions is about more than corruption and failure. Revolutions in technology mean younger people are less dependent on institutions and are more personally empowered. Americans now older than sixty likely graduated from high school or college and focused on finding a job with a company, ideally a medium or large institution. They may have thought about a long-term career with that company because of its good benefits and solid retirement plan.

That is not how young people think anymore. One poll found that 6 out of 10 college students plan to start their own business.[6] I thought that statistic was ludicrous until I remembered that I started a business before graduating from seminary, and I've started three more since then.

This is a highly entreprenuerial generation that carries a profound distrust of institutions. And these same values carry over into their faith. In their pursuit of Christ, they are not thinking about committing themselves to a single institutional church. They're happy to get their Bible teaching from Tim Keller's podcast. They'll serve with that World Relief or International Justice Mission program in the city. They'll study that Francis Chan book with some friends on Wednesday nights or take in that Taizé worship service once a month at the cathedral in Oak Park. But commit to one local church? No thanks.

The Over-Institutional Church

That's a glimpse of what's happening in our culture. We are seeing the emergence of an anti-institutional, highly entrepreneurial generation. Now we have to look at the other side—what's happening within American churches that might be contributing to the dropout trend.

In Ephesians 4, the apostle Paul gives us a vision for how the church is supposed to function. Once we grasp God's intention for the church, we can begin to recognize how we stray and construct vampire churches instead.

Paul begins by writing about our unity in God, but then he goes on to describe our diversity. "Grace was given to each one of us according to the measure of Christ's gift" (Eph. 4:7). He then quotes Psalm 68, "Therefore it says, 'When he ascended on high he led a host of captives, and he gave gifts to men'" (Eph. 4:8). Paul is speaking of Jesus' victory at the resurrection and His ascension into heaven. Like a king returning from a victorious battle, He bestows the spoils of war on His people.

Paul continues, "In saying, 'He ascended,' what does it mean but that he had also descended into the lower regions, the earth? He who descended is the one who also ascended far above all the heavens, that he might fill all things" (Eph. 4:9–10). This is important and often overlooked when studying God's vision for the church. Paul says that Jesus' goal in descending to the earth through His incarnation and ascending to heaven after His resurrection as the victorious King is to "fill all things." Simply put, Jesus' mission is to rule over everything.

In light of this, Paul says that Jesus has given people to the church as gifts: "And he gave the apostles, the prophets, the evangelists, the shepherds and teachers . . ." (Eph. 4:11). In other letters Paul writes about spiritual gifts as functions, like teaching, healing, prophecy, and hospitality, but he does something different in Ephesians. Rather than list behaviors, he lists people. Paul says Christ has given his church the gift of leaders: apostles, prophets, evangelists, teachers, and shepherds for an important purpose: ". . . to equip the saints for the work of ministry" (Eph. 4:12).

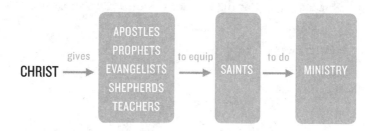

We have another language challenge in this verse. Like the word *church*, the word *ministry* is terribly misused in our culture. Today it is popularly used to mean religious work or activities. Pastors do ministry; plumbers do not. Missionaries do ministry; mechanics do not. When a volunteer leads a Bible study, that is ministry; when a volunteer leads a sci-fi book club, that is not. We define ministry as church work.

That is not what Paul meant.

First of all, in Paul's day there were no church buildings or 501(c)(3) ministries, and the word *ministry* did not refer to the activity of a certain vocation or class of people.

Instead, it referred to any act of service that brought glory to God. To really grasp Paul's point here, we need to look back at the context. Paul places the discussion of Christ's gifts to the church, leaders, and their task of equipping the saints within the larger, cosmic mission of Jesus to rule over everything. The question Paul is addressing here is, *How does Jesus extend His rule over all things?* The answer: By giving the church leaders, filled with His power, to equip His people to serve Him and manifest His rule everywhere.

Not just inside a church building.

Not merely under the banner of nonprofit ministries.

Not simply on Sundays.

Leaders within the church are called to equip us to serve Jesus everywhere, every day, and in every aspect of our lives.

Ephesians 4

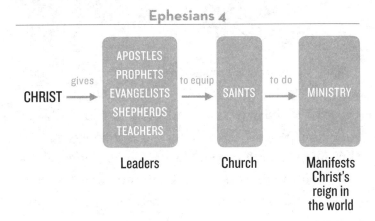

CHRIST	gives	APOSTLES PROPHETS EVANGELISTS SHEPHERDS TEACHERS	to equip	SAINTS	to do	MINISTRY
		Leaders		Church		Manifests Christ's reign in the world

I find this vision of the church and its leadership beautiful and compelling. I also find it liberating.

But here's the problem—this vision from Ephesians 4 does not represent the dominant philosophy of ministry now active in Church, Inc. The model I was taught in seminary, and that gets extolled at most ministry conferences and in the pages of church-growth books, looks more like this:

Vampire Church

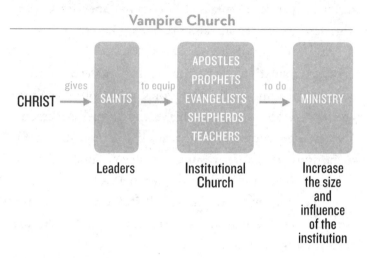

This is what I call a *vampire church*, and it is predicated on a misunderstanding of Jesus' mission and the meaning of ministry. It assumes that Jesus' goal is to simply reign over the church while all other aspects of His creation are relegated to irrelevance. This view assumes our Lord created the universe and then retired into full-time church work. Therefore, the vocations of God's people in business, government, the arts, education, the home, the social sector, and the media are rarely, if ever, acknowledged or affirmed by Church, Inc., and they are certainly not celebrated as genuine callings from God.

Rather than empowering people to manifest God's reign in the world, vampire churches seek to use people to advance the goals of the institutional church. Success, therefore, is reached when a person is plugged into the apparatus of the church institution rather than released to serve God's people and their neighbors out in the world, through their vocations, and in communion with Christ. This drive to use people rather than empower them is what drains the life out of them.

The combination of a vampire church model of ministry and the emerging, anti-institutional values of our culture creates a perfect storm leading to church disengagement. We have a generation of Americans that is more distrustful of institutions than any since the Revolution, and we're seeing a model of church leadership that is highly institutionalized and inwardly focused. Is it any wonder young people, even those committed to Christ, aren't pouring their lives into the local church?

A few years ago, my colleagues at *Leadership Journal* and I organized a pastor listening tour. It was our chance to hear what pastors around the country are struggling with and what their churches need help with. I had one conversation with a church planter that was fascinating. He was about my age, but far cooler, which isn't difficult. I asked him, "What's the biggest challenge you're facing?"

Without a moment of reflection he said, "How do I get a generation that doesn't believe in commitment to commit to the church?"

My first thought was, *What does he mean by the word church*? It turned out a significant number of young adults were engaging with his community through support groups, Bible studies, and in relationships with one another. The problem was, according to the pastor, they were not "stepping up" with their time and money to support the institution. So I asked, "What are you asking them to do?"

The pastor explained the myriad of ministry programs he wanted to launch—outreach initiatives, service projects, international mission partnerships—but these young people were not committing to them. No doubt many other pastors can relate to his frustration.

But here's the part I couldn't reconcile. I'd spent a lot of time in that pastor's city over the preceding years. I couldn't think of a city in the United States that had more committed, engaged, and active young Christians. We profiled many of their stories in our flagship magazine, *Christianity Today*. They were doing remarkable things throughout their community and in every channel of the culture to end human trafficking, support the homeless, run afterschool programs, build bridges of healing and understanding between the church and LGBT communities, and bring beauty and art into the poorest neighborhoods. I even met young Christians there operating food trucks and serving pizza with a clear sense of calling from God and a missional mindset.

This pastor was upset that young Christians weren't committed to the institutional agenda of his church, and his conclusion was that they must not be committed to Christ. But what if it's the opposite? What if the problem isn't that young people aren't committed to the church, but that the church isn't committed to young people? I challenged him with a different approach: rather than trying

> The greatest resource God has given this planet are His redeemed and Spirit-filled people. Our job is not to collect and protect them like animals in a zoo, but to equip and release them into the wild of the world.

to get young people to engage your institution's programs and goals, what if you shifted the institution to equip young people to better accomplish what God is calling them to do in the world? Based on his blank stare, I don't think he bought my idea.

What's so encouraging to me, however, is that there are leaders who are making the shift away from a vampire model of church. They see the disconnect between Church, Inc. and what Paul describes in Ephesians 4. There are institutional churches shifting their thinking from using people to empowering people. From growing the institution to growing disciples. From measuring how many people come to a service on Sunday to how many are manifesting the reign of Christ Monday through Saturday in every sector of their community.

I've met many of those pastors as well, and what's even more encouraging is meeting the people of their churches who feel affirmed and equipped. The greatest resource God has given this planet are His redeemed and Spirit-filled people. Our job is not to collect and protect them like animals in a zoo, but to equip and release them into the wild of the world.

There is hope.

As leaders, if we are to avoid building vampire churches, we must remember these three things:

1. The church is the community of God's redeemed and empowered people.

2. The church institution exists to equip God's people. God's people do not exist to equip the institution.

3. Ministry is not limited to what we do within the church institution, but should include what we do to manifest the reign of Christ in the world.

A few years ago, I interviewed Dallas Willard. We talked about many of the dysfunctions within the modern church, including some of what I've covered above. Dallas, I think it's fair to say, recognized the problems and their deeper causes more clearly than I did. At the end of that two-hour conversation, I asked him, "When you look at how off track we are, do you ever just throw up your hands in despair?"

He smiled at me and said, "Never."

"How can you not?" I asked. "You just spent two hours explaining everything that's wrong with the church."

"Because," he said, "I know Christ is the head of His church and He knows what He's doing."

The church is facing many challenges in our culture; I've touched on just a few above. Our response to these challenges shouldn't be to roll out an elaborate new program or grasp at what marketing experts say is the next hot trend. Nor should it be pointing an accusing finger at our increasingly secular culture, or wagging a judgmental finger at the institutional church.

The answer is for us, the church, the people of Christ, to align ourselves more closely to Christ and His Word, to remember our callings to one another and to this world, and to manifest the reign of Christ, who has been raised up and is seated at the right hand of the Father and who, even now, is making all things new. We do not lose hope, because He is still the head of His church, and the gates of hell will not prevail against it.

REFLECTION AND APPLICATION

After talking with dozens of pastors who have moved away from the vampire-church model, I found that they all engage in a common practice—pastoral workplace visitation. They regularly get outside the church to engage members where they work. This, of course, was commonplace in ministry before the age of Church, Inc. Today, however, most of us stay in the church office and expect the sheep to come to us. Set aside regular time to meet those you serve in their contexts. Learn about their work, callings, and environments. This is certain to transform how you see your people and equip them for the life Christ has called them to.

As you consider the four definitions of church, which one fills your thoughts and imagination? Which "church" are you most preoccupied with? What would help you shift your focus away from the institutional structures and rediscover the primary importance of God's people once again?

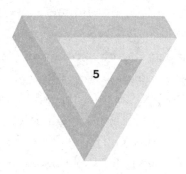

5

SHEPHERDS

SHEEP ARE STUPID. Consider news that came from Turkey in 2005. People from the town of Gevas watched in horror as one sheep jumped to its death, and then 1,500 more followed after. When the villagers, whose livelihoods depended on the flock, arrived at the bottom of the mountain, they found a billowy white pile of death. In all, 450 sheep were lost, but amazingly the rest had survived. It seems that as the pile grew higher, the fall was more cushioned. Why did these sheep perish? It turns out the shepherds responsible for protecting the flock had left the sheep on the mountain and had gone to eat breakfast when the fleeces started to fly.

The importance of a shepherd is inversely proportional to the intelligence of the animal. Dogs, for example, manage to survive fairly well even without a human overseer. Dolphins do even better. Sheep, on the other hand, don't have the good sense not to jump off a cliff. They need a shepherd to survive.

The fact that Scripture often compares God's people to sheep ought to humble us. We need godly shepherds to lead, feed, and protect us from the world and from ourselves. We are irrefutably sinful (and often stupid) creatures, willing to throw ourselves off a cliff of self-destruction. This truth about God's sheep, however, can tempt shepherds to overstep their role. Sometimes the most difficult part about pastoral ministry is knowing what is not our responsibility.

After the resurrection, Jesus restores Peter and calls him to shepherd His flock. Three times Jesus calls Peter to "feed" or "tend" His sheep and concludes with an allusion to his eventual martyrdom. Perhaps Peter was less than thrilled with this assignment, because he immediately notices John and asks Jesus about John's calling. The Lord swiftly rebukes him: "If it is my will that he remain until I come, what is that to you? You follow me!" (John 21:22).

In this story we see Peter's temptation to overstep his role. He wants to know, and perhaps influence, John's calling. But Jesus makes it clear that Peter's responsibility is not to call. Essentially, Jesus says, "You feed. You tend. You do not call. That is My prerogative. You are the servant; I am the Master."

This has always been the temptation for shepherds. Knowing how helpless and stupid sheep can be, we come to believe that without our guidance they can do nothing. So beyond feeding and tending, we assume it is also our responsibility to call, to tell Christ's sheep what they are to do. We believe this because it is partially true. Feeding and tending includes teaching. We are to instruct God's flock from Scripture and teach them to obey all He has commanded. The general commands from the Bible that apply to all disciples are sometimes known as our *corporate* or *common* calling.

Where we overstep as shepherds is when we assume the responsibility for a disciple's specific calling. This is what Peter attempted to do with John, and it's a tendency our culture's understanding of leadership often encourages. In corporate America, the leader is the person with the vision. She then calls others to a single task and sets forth accomplishing it. We've accepted this view of leadership within the church, too. We often believe the pastor's role is to articulate a vision from God and call all people to that single work. Success is then measured by how many people answer our call.

We spend much of our energy calling people to our mission—to advance our church, to be evangelists or, even better, missionaries—and we do this with the best of intentions. We want to see God's work accomplished. What we forget is that Christ has called us to be shepherds who feed and tend, not masters who call. That is His job; the sheep are, after all, His. Even in Matthew 9, when Jesus says, "The harvest is plentiful, but the laborers are few," He does not tell His disciples to find, call, and send out more laborers. He instructs them to "pray earnestly to the Lord of the harvest to send out laborers." Jesus does not outsource to us God's responsibility to call.

Our instinct to protect the sheep under our care is a good one; heaven knows they need someone to keep them safe. But when feeding and tending becomes controlling, we've overstepped our role as a shepherd. We may think it's our job to call as many people into ministry, missions, or church work as possible, but a disciple's specific calling always comes from Christ. Our task is to lead disciples into deeper communion with Him. Christ's sheep need a shepherd. They already have a Lord.

REFLECTION AND APPLICATION

What responsibilities do you feel that rightly belong only to the Holy Spirit? How are you seeking to control the specific callings of the sheep entrusted to your care?

In what ways have the values of businesses and corporations become integrated into your ministry? Which of these values are genuinely helpful, and which may be drawing you from the ways of Christ?

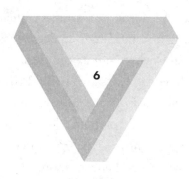

6

DRAMAS

AT ANY GIVEN MOMENT, we are each engaged in three dramas, but ultimately only one of them matters.

First, there is the drama of the practical. These are the events and measurable conditions that surround us every day. For many church leaders, the current drama of the practical involves keeping their ministries solvent with enough of the ABCs—attenders, buildings, and cash. Sometimes it moves into more lofty concerns that are nonetheless practical, like how to win younger members or strategically restructure a leadership team or discipleship ministry. Those men and women who learn to master the drama of the practical are often the most revered and celebrated. They know how to get things done, so we buy their books, attend their conferences, and listen to their advice.

But there is a second drama that many practical actors ignore: the drama of the theoretical. While we are busy living our lives and doing our ministry, there is a deeper drama informing and guiding our decisions. This drama of the theoretical is where our assumptions and beliefs exert invisible influence. They lurk behind the scenes, pulling the levers and pushing the buttons that animate our practical decisions, and for many leaders these shadowy forces are never brought into the light or challenged. They include what we really believe about the church, mission, culture, and theology. Those with more reflective faculties and a greater dose of self-awareness are able to speak to and identify this drama of the theoretical in a way mere practical dramatists cannot. For this reason, as my college professor used to say, they often find themselves writing about the world rather than running it.

> We are not merely managers of religious institutions with practical duties. Neither are we merely thought-leaders living on the rarified air of theory and vision.

Most pastors and church leaders, as well as the resources created to help them, are primarily concerned with these two dramas—the practical and the theoretical. What should I do and what should I think? But we deceive ourselves if we believe these two dramas comprise the bulk of our life or motivation. Because behind the drama of the practical, and far deeper than the drama of the theoretical, there lies a third drama more powerful than either, and whose silent movements control them both—the drama of the eternal.

The Quaker missionary and scholar Thomas Kelly wrote about this deeper drama as World War II was escalating:

> Out in front of us is the drama of men and of nations, seething, struggling, laboring, dying. Upon this tragic drama in these days our eyes are all set in anxious watchfulness and in prayer. But within the silences of the souls of men an eternal drama is ever being enacted, in these days as well as in others. And on the outcome of this inner drama rests, ultimately, the outer pageant of history. It is the drama of the Hound of Heaven baying relentlessly upon the track of man.[1]

We are not merely managers of religious institutions with practical duties. Neither are we merely thought-leaders living on the rarified air of theory and vision. We are spiritual leaders called to shepherd the souls of women, men, and children. Of all people, we are called to be most aware and sensitive to the drama of the eternal, and yet I hear so little about this responsibility among church leaders today. If we, the leaders of Christ's church, will not take up this responsibility, then who will?

Of course, long before we can hope to see into the "silences of the souls of men," we must learn to discern the secret things that move within our own souls. I recall moderating a conversation among pastors debating the merits of "missional" versus "attractional" church models. It was an exercise in the drama of the theoretical. All the while, however, I suspected that matters deeper than theory were driving each argument. Were the pastors aware of the impulses of their souls? Am I? Can we see how our dedication to one model or the other is linked to the eternal drama at play deeper within? What does attracting a crowd to hear me speak do to satisfy my insecure identity? How might an aggressively missional model fuel my need for accomplishment? We are naïve to think the drama of the eternal isn't in some way directing the drama of the theoretical.

Likewise, our energetic and often frenzied pace in ministry (the drama of the practical) finds its headwaters in the drama of the eternal. Do our actions, even the busy ones, flow from a soul at peace in the presence of the Lord, or are we accomplishing objectives from an idolatrous desire to serve our ego? The resolution of this inner drama, as Thomas Kelly remarks, will ultimately determine the outer pageant of our lives and ministries.

Consider the tragically common story of successful pastors living double lives. Ted Haggard, former pastor of New Life Church and president of the National Association of Evangelicals, had a very public implosion in 2006, just as my church was recovering from its own leadership scandal. The mess in my congregation was too close for me to recognize the hidden dramas at work, but I was far enough removed from Haggard that his story became instructive. By any measure, Haggard was an expert in the drama of the practical—he grew a very large church. Likewise, many celebrated his ability to engage the drama of the theoretical—he became a leader in the evangelical political and cultural movement. Ultimately, however, it was the drama of the eternal in his soul that defined his destiny. Watching that unfold left me to wonder, could the very same wound in Haggard's soul that led to drug abuse and sexual misconduct have also fueled his celebrated ministry achievements? Could practical ministry success and painful failure germinate from the same seed?

If we take our gaze off the celebrity pastors (practical dramatists) and the ministry pundits (theoretical dramatists) and fix our eyes once again on Jesus, we'll discover a spiritual leader with the wisdom to focus on the only drama that really matters. Jesus lived and served from a soul at one with the Father and an identity secure in His love. From this inner place He drew the strength to do mighty works (drama of the practical) and teach profound truths (drama of the theoretical), but more importantly He found the courage to endure outward failure, ridicule, and abandonment. The drama of the eternal, His inner communion with the Father, defined and determined the outward drama of His life. Unfortunately, too many of us in ministry have it the other way around.

At any given moment, we are each engaged in three dramas, but ultimately only one of them matters.

Read the spiritual classic by Brother Lawrence, *The Practice of the Presence of God*. Consider what it would look like in your life to pray without ceasing and live with a constant awareness of the Lord's presence.

Church, Inc. celebrates measurable results, but how does your ministry validate and encourage people who seek the less visible deepening of their communion with God? What can you do to elevate the importance of this drama in your community?

7

ENEMIES

IT'S NOT JUST HUMANS who like to congregate at my church. The small lawn between the building and parking lot attracts Canada geese. For those of you unfamiliar with the species, or who are blessed to live in a region beyond their imperial ambitions, allow me to explain. Canada geese are evil.

They swoop in like alien invaders and occupy a community's recreational areas—golf courses, parks, playing fields, you name it. At first their presence is viewed as benign, particularly as their little goslings add a storybook charm to the scene. But these are not graceful swans or passive ducks. Draw too near and the birds extend their wings, lower their heads, and release an unholy hiss like a fell beast of Mordor. If the warning is unheeded, they will charge and attack with astonishing speed—something I witnessed firsthand in high school as a friend on rollerblades nearly lost his ear to a rogue goose. With their lifeless black eyes and taste for blood, Canada geese are the Great Whites of suburbia.

Why are they attracted to my church? I cannot say for certain. But the presence of these demon birds (I'm convinced they were the inspiration for Alfred Hitchcock's film) illustrates something about the spiritual enemy with whom we contend. Like the unseen "powers and authorities" the apostle Paul says we strive against (Eph. 6:12), the geese are not always visible on Sunday mornings. But their presence is still felt by all as we dodge their copious droppings on the sidewalk. Every week as we prepared to exit our minivan, my four-year-old daughter would pause to remind us of the danger: "We're going to church. Watch out for poop." Indeed, I would say to myself.

In many church communities, talk about spiritual powers is uncommon. Some have dismissed it as residue of an antiquated worldview, like believing the sun orbits the earth. Others avoid the topic because it may be uncomfortable for newcomers or associated with unflattering portrayals of Christianity in popular culture. For many reasons, church leaders may passively deny the role of spiritual authorities, and we may not acknowledge their opposition in our work. But like the unseen geese at my church, we cannot deny the evidence of their presence.

Like the minefield of poop that is our church parking lot, our communities are littered with the debris left by destructive spiritual forces: divorce, addiction, injustice, racism, materialism, dishonesty, abuse. If your community is soiled by any of these (and how could it not be?), you are engaged in a spiritual battle with unseen forces. Remember, the New Testament doesn't just present spiritual warfare as a cinematic battle between angels and demons. Scripture speaks about the systems of "the world" as corrupt and destructive. In other words, spiritual battle isn't just with demons, but with dehumanizing systems, too. For Paul they are one and the same.

That means it will require far more than human intelligence and devices to overcome these forces. We cannot program our curriculum or teach our way to victory over any of them because these maladies were not caused by human ignorance or villainy alone. President Kennedy famously said, "Our problems are man-made; therefore, they may be solved by man." The apostle Paul disagrees. He reminds us that we "do not wrestle against flesh and blood, but against . . . spiritual forces" (Eph. 6:12). Therefore we require spiritual weapons.

This does not mean we have no active role to play or that we should not employ human intelligence in our work. Rather, it means that we humbly recognize the truth that we need a power far greater than our own to overcome. Perhaps this is why Paul lists truth as the first element of the "armor of God" in Ephesians 6. Everything begins with seeing the truth about our enemy, acknowledging the truth about ourselves, and humbly admitting the truth that we need God's help.

Our failure to see the truth about ourselves and our enemy may explain why so few pastors value prayer these days. A survey by Barna asked church leaders from a spectrum of denominational backgrounds to list their church's highest priorities. Of the twelve areas of ministry listed, prayer came in dead last, with only 3 percent of pastors identifying it as a priority.[1] Do we agree with Kennedy's delusion that we can overcome what opposes us through human power alone? Have we dismissed Paul as a premodern minister with a misplaced trust in prayer?

We have an enemy that is active and cunning. Rather than arguing about the theological question of whether this enemy resides in a personal demonic presence or the corrosive power of the world's system (and why can't it be both?), we should be asking God to help us see the terrible effects of this enemy among our people. Whatever the precise source, when we acknowledge that the excrement in our church is no less vile than in the surrounding community, it should humble us to see that we need a power beyond ourselves to overcome it. We need grace. We need to access this grace through prayer. And when that truth is embraced, our enemy will tremble.

REFLECTION AND APPLICATION

What makes your church or ministry different from a non-Christian nonprofit organization? Would an outside observer recognize practices or behaviors that would identity your work as uniquely Christian? And how does your approach to work acknowledge the reality of spiritual forces, not merely natural ones?

Most ministries have a financial budgeting and audit process. Why don't we have a prayer audit? Rather than being an afterthought or tacked-on element to a gathering, what would it look like to make prayer an indispensable component of your work and community?

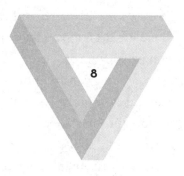

8

SIMPLICITY

ORDERING A COFFEE used to mean answering two questions: "Regular or decaf?" and "Black or cream and sugar?" Today Starbucks offers over eighty-seven thousand different drink combinations. For decades marketing gurus have said people want choices because customization empowers the individual, but when facing a menu with thousands of drink choices, some feel overwhelmed rather than empowered. Psychologists call this the "tyranny of choice," and it explains why the value of simplicity is on the rise.

As our society becomes more complex, people are drawn to the simple. We see it in the success of Apple devices with their austere designs and ease of use. A new generation of fast food companies has emerged, rejecting McDonald's "something for everyone" menu. The plain "urban prairie" architecture of Chipotle restaurants, for example, matches the simplicity of its menu.

It appears the call to simplify has been heard by church leaders as well. There has been a parade of ministry books published celebrating the virtues of "lean," "small," "simple," and "nimble" church, and the construction of larger church buildings is at an all-time low in the United States—a trend that started well before the Great Recession.[1] The glamour of the mega-ministry and its ability to offer greater choices appears to be fading, at least in some regions. But is this shift anything more than a reflection of social trends?

I suspect that changing social values play a part. As I discussed in an earlier chapter, research shows that Millennials are suspicious of large institutions, unlike Baby Boomers, who usually equate largeness with legitimacy. Still, I wonder if we're also witnessing a theological shift that is eroding the philosophical foundations of very large ministries (VLMs) while providing validation for leaner ones.

Part of why VLMs emerge is the implicit belief in a sacred/secular divide. This view holds that the world is split into that which God cares about (sacred) and that which is ultimately unimportant (secular). Accounting, for example, is secular work without any eternal value, but doing accounting for a church—well, now you're counting beans for the kingdom of God. Rather than affirming the work of Christians serving as counselors, mechanics, or fitness trainers out in the community, these activities only find validation when they are incorporated into ministries. Over time this desire to sanctify our work results in VLMs housing restaurants, auto repair shops, fitness centers, retail stores, clinics, and a plethora of programs requiring a steady influx of volunteers to manage.

The sacred/secular divide that dominated the Middle Ages is what led, in part, to the massive institutional expansion of the Roman Catholic Church. Every sphere of culture—government, the arts, education, commerce, etc.—was sanctified by coming under the church's control and into its institutional structure.

It wasn't until the Reformation, and its dismantling of the wall between sacred and secular, that things began to change. Luther, Calvin, and their spiritual descendants affirmed a theology of vocation that said all of life, and all work, were sacred. Accounting mattered and brought glory to God even when done outside the church. This allowed the institutional church to shrink its footprint and simplify its ministry to preaching the Scriptures and administering the sacraments. It also empowered the laity to carry Christ's presence into the various channels of the culture through their vocations, rather than forcing the entire culture under the domain of the institutional church.

I suspect something similar is taking hold in the North American church today. After living with an assumed sacred/secular divide for decades and the resulting proliferation of VLMs, many are now questioning the divide. A new generation of church leaders and laity are restoring a vision for cultural participation and a renewed theology of vocation. They're coming to see the value of their lives, work, and social engagement without the need to be a "ministry" or to be under the banner of an institutional church.

The side effect is a new freedom for ministers to be pastors again rather than CEOs. When the laity is empowered and their vocations in the world are validated, those of us called to shepherd God's people can abandon the pressure to grow and manage a VLM and instead focus on our call to teach the Bible and administer the sacraments.

It seems like a paradox, but we can actually focus more on ministry if we would focus less on ministry. By that I mean using every opportunity to publicly affirm the important callings Christ has given to members of the church in the world. Rather than using another ministry-focused illustration in the sermon, why not highlight a story from another profession represented in the congregation? Rather than only laying hands upon and praying for ministers and missionaries, why not invite educators up at the start of the semester and pray that God would bless their important work? Rather than having your next church board meeting in the fellowship hall, why not meet at the workplace of a board member and provide a few minutes for her to share about her calling?

When auto mechanics, accountants, health-care workers, and horticulturists come to see their work as part of what God is doing in the world, and when it is genuinely validated by pastors, there will be less demand for these things to exist within the structure of the church. This, in turn, allows pastors to be pastors again rather than auto mechanics, accountants, health-care workers, or horticulturists. That is a simple vision of the church many of us are ready for.

What is measured and celebrated in your ministry community? What does this reveal about what you value and what you don't? How are you unknowingly perpetuating the false categories of "sacred" and "secular"?

With your leadership team, begin a discussion about what can be simplified in your structure. How does the existing complexity keep God's people occupied inside the structures of the organization rather than engaging the world He loves outside?

COMPLEXITY

SOMETIMES WE FIND wisdom in unexpected places—like in Frank Zappa's autobiography. He wrote this wonderful little paragraph titled "Death by Nostalgia."

> *It isn't necessary to imagine the world ending in fire or ice—there are two other possibilities: one is paper-work, and the other is nostalgia. When you compute the length of time between* **The Event** *and* **The Nostalgia For The Event**, *the span seems to be about* **a year less in each cycle.** *Eventually, within the next quarter of a century the nostalgia cycles will be so close together that people will not be able to take a step without being nostalgic for the one they just took. At that point, everything stops. Death by Nostalgia.*[1]

I wonder if Frank Zappa's diagnosis applies to the evangelical movement as well. As the world becomes more confusing and our mission faces unforeseen obstacles, we are tempted to look back at how wonderful things used to be. Nostalgia causes us to lament the complexity of the present and idealize the false simplicity of the past. In this chapter we'll explore how simple ministry used to be, how it's become much more complicated, and the blessings hidden in that change. To begin, we need to recognize three ways our mission seemed less complicated in the past.

The Simple Past

First, in the past there was a general consensus among evangelicals that evangelism, and global missions in particular, was of paramount importance. This was advanced in no small part by a particular eschatology from the nineteenth century that was popularized after World War I. It said that this earth and all of creation were doomed for destruction, and that the only things to endure for eternity were the souls of the redeemed. This dualistic, even gnostic, vision of the world that dismissed the material and elevated the immaterial made it clear that the only work of ultimate importance was the work of saving souls—missions.

Second, in the past this elevation of ministry (and diminishment of other vocations) attracted Christians, particularly those seeking significance, into ministry. But to actually engage that calling and fulfill their desire to make an impact in the world, Christians relied on institutions. Denominations and parachurch organizations flourished because they were absolutely necessary to connect the individual to their calling.

Third, in the past, mission-sending organizations could rely on the local church as a partner in this work. They knew that a child raised in an evangelical church would be taught the Bible, carry a Christian worldview, and by the time he or she graduated from high school or college, be reasonably prepared with a foundation of Christian faith to carry the mission forward.

So, in the past we had what appeared to be a relatively simple model for missions. The local church prepared a person, a dualistic eschatology motivated a person, and a denomination or parachurch institution deployed a person to the mission field. Because of this reliable formula, evangelical missions organizations grew throughout much of the twentieth century. They recruited more people and sent more of them overseas. The simple system worked.

The Complicated Present

But then things started getting complicated. A new generation grew up, my generation, and we began to see the world and God's mission differently. I am a member of Generation X—or what I prefer to call the "Jumbo Jet Generation." Mine is the first generation to grow up amid rapid globalization, and it fundamentally changed the way we see the world and our place within it.

In 1970 the Boeing 747, commonly called the Jumbo

Jet, entered service. It was the largest, most economical commercial airliner ever built. For the first time, intercontinental travel became affordable for millions of people. The 747 inaugurated an era of unprecedented cultural mixing. I could not have existed in a world before the Jumbo Jet, because its lower travel costs made it possible for a twenty-four-year-old nurse from Chicago to fly to Bombay, where she fell in love with a twenty-eight-year-old doctor. And here I am. By the time I graduated from high school, I had visited thirty foreign countries.

I realize most of my peers didn't travel as much as I did, but they also grew up in a more complicated world. Since the Jumbo Jet entered service, more people have immigrated to the United States through LAX and JFK than ever passed through Ellis Island. By the 1980s it was clear that the world was coming to us. People of all faiths and cultures were in our neighborhoods and in our schools, and we saw the suffering of the world in our family rooms with the advent of live global television. We saw the tanks roll into Tiananmen Square, and we saw the images of famine in Ethiopia as Michael Jackson led us to sing, "We Are the World."

I am convinced that this global perspective contributed to a shift in our eschatology. Younger Christians are increasingly rejecting the dualism that says the material world doesn't ultimately matter. Therefore, a missiology that elevates gospel proclamation over gospel demonstration doesn't resonate with us. Instead, more voices are driving a movement in the church to elevate the value of callings beyond ministry, including the arts, science, government, business, education, the social sector, the media, and the home. In other words, the message that only evangelism matters doesn't work like it used to because a generation with global exposure carries global concerns that require global responses. In many parts of the church, therefore, it isn't the missionary who is most celebrated today, but the social activist—a pendulum swing with its own blindness and problems.

Here's the second thing that's happened to my generation: we grew up with ubiquitous entertainment. From Sesame Street to MTV, from Walkmans to iPods, we refuse to be bored, and never-ending media engagement has formed us to have the attention spans of caffeinated gold fish. That's not a joke. Research has shown that in the last fifteen years, the average American's attention span has decreased from twelve seconds to eight, which is one second less than a goldfish's.[2] That means to keep us engaged, local churches have become more and more like theaters and less and less like schools. Despite an explosion in the number of megachurches and Christian radio stations in the last forty years, statistics show younger evangelicals know less about the Bible and are less likely to have a Christian worldview than their parents. Church is more fun but less formative than ever before.

Not long ago, I met with the president of a respected Christian college to discuss the challenges his school is facing. He said that in the past he could safely assume that a freshman coming from a Christian family and an evangelical church knew the Bible and held the basic framework of a Christian worldview. Today, however, that is no longer true, and it is causing real problems for the college. "This institution," he said, "wasn't designed to take the place of the local church." Students simply aren't prepared for a Christian liberal arts education because they aren't rooted in Christian faith. I've heard very similar struggles from the leaders of mission agencies. Many of these parachurch operations were not designed to do the foundational work of basic discipleship. They assumed that was the local church's job. That assumption is no longer safe.

Finally, my generation was the first one born after the legalization and broad acceptance of no-fault divorce. With it, the brokenness and disunity that have always existed in the world came into our homes and into our families as never before. We have always known the world to be an unsafe place, but we were the first generation of Americans to experience that reality at the most intimate, identity-forming level. The broken promises of our parents to each other and to us left us jaded and cynical—not just toward marriage, but toward every institution in our culture. Longitudinal studies by Gallup show that our confidence in schools, government, businesses, the military, the police, and the church have all declined dramatically since the 1970s.[3]

All of this means the familiar, simple system of preparing, motivating, and deploying Christians for the mission that worked in the past has become much, much more complicated. We are no longer motivated by a simple eschatology that says only evangelism ultimately matters. We are no longer prepared by the local church to advance that mission. And we are less likely to trust denominational or parachurch institutions to deploy us on that mission.

What seemed simple in the past is now complex, and it has made some of us the victims of nostalgia. We are reluctant to change our models or systems. We blame local churches—an easy target—for failing to support missions. We rely on an aging demographic of donors who are equally (and maybe more) nostalgic as we are for the way missions used to be, rather than cultivate new sources of revenue. All of this is a prescription for death by nostalgia.

Responding to Complexity

But we do not have to despair over the changes we are seeing. There is always the opportunity for a hopeful and faithful response, and an example is given to us in Numbers 11. Moses had been leading the Israelites through the wilderness, but the burden of leadership was heavy on him, and he cried out to the Lord for help. In response, the Lord gave Moses a plan, which he followed:

> [Moses] gathered seventy men of the elders of the people and placed them around the tent. Then the LORD came down in the cloud and spoke to him, and took some of the Spirit that was on him and put it on the seventy elders. And as soon as the Spirit rested on them, they prophesied.
> (vv. 24–25)

The mantle of leadership that Moses carried was now shared by seventy others. But here's the interesting part:

> Now two men remained in the camp, one named Eldad, and the other named Medad, and the Spirit rested on them. They were among those registered, but they had not gone out to the tent, and so they prophesied in the camp. And a young man ran and told Moses, "Eldad and Medad are prophesying in the camp." And Joshua the son of Nun, the assistant of Moses from his youth, said, "My lord Moses, stop them." But Moses said to him, "Are you jealous for my sake? Would that all the LORD's people were prophets, that the LORD would put his Spirit on them!" (Num. 11:26–29)

Before this moment, it was understood that God spoke through Moses alone. It was a simple line of communication: from the Lord, through Moses, to the people. This story also occurs not long after God gave the people His laws—very clear and strict commandments outlining precisely how things were to be done, including procedures for sacrifices, cleansing, and atonement for sins. Things were clear. Things were simple. Perhaps most relevant for this story, it's important to remember that it was God Himself who gave the order for the seventy elders to leave the camp and gather at the tabernacle to receive the Spirit.

Eldad and Medad, however, didn't stick to the plan. They didn't leave the camp and gather at the tabernacle. But the Spirit came upon them anyway. God appeared to be doing something inconsistent with His own simple instructions. Things were suddenly more complicated. This results in both fear and anger among the people. First, a young man runs to tell Moses about these men who appear to be violating his command, and then Joshua is outraged and wants Eldad and Medad punished immediately.

Can you relate? When things are no longer "the way they're supposed to be" or "the way they used to be," we become afraid. We become angry. Like Joshua, we want things put back in proper order. We want to return to the simple, linear, recongnizable way of operating because the old system made sense. What I want you to see, however, are the different responses to this unexpected complication from Moses and Joshua. Joshua reacts to these new complications in fear, alarm, and anger. Moses, however, sees things very differently.

Complexity shatters our illusion of control.

We worship a God of surprises. He surprised Moses and Joshua by working even outside His own instructions—and that is a theme we see throughout Scripture. If the Bible and history have taught us anything, it's that God is notoriously uncooperative at our attempts at controlling Him. We want to contain Him, institutionalize Him, and systematize Him so that we can ultimately understand, predict, and control Him. So, when the Lord does something unexpected, when He complicates our life or our world, it's a reminder that control is an illusion. We never had it, and we never will. That awareness is a gift.

When my daughter Lucy was a toddler, she was our most mischievous kid, and her favorite game involved the dog food. She'd sneak over to the dog's dish and throw the food all over the kitchen. Sometimes I'd catch her heading to the bowl, about to put her hands in. "Lucy!" I'd say. She'd freeze and look over at me. "Don't you touch that dog food." She'd look at me, smile, throw the food as fast as she could and run out of the kitchen giggling.

After that happened a few times, it finally occurred to me that it wasn't throwing the dog food that she liked so much. It was my reaction. She liked making me upset. That was the payoff for her.

Sometimes God is mischievous like that. He likes throwing dog food all over the kitchen of our lives. What we like to keep contained and tidy and under control, He throws up in the air—and He does it because He wants to get a reaction out of us. He does it to teach us a lesson, to show us that we are not in control, and that any sense of control we do have is just an illusion.

Thomas Aquinas was the greatest theologian of the Middle Ages. His *Summa Theologica* answered ten thousand objections to the Christian faith; it's considered one of the greatest intellectual achievements of Western civilization. Aquinas took the mysteries and complexities of God and faith and systematically simplified them for human understanding. But on December 6, 1273, he abruptly announced that he would write no more. While worshiping in the chapel that day, Aquinas had an intense, unexpected experience with God that shattered his categories. "I can do no more," he said. "Such things have been revealed to me that all I have written seem to me to be straw."

When the illusion of our control is shattered, when we are confronted with the complexity of reality, we are humbled. Today, much of the evangelical church is losing its illusion of control. God is throwing the dog food we've kept in the bowl for a century all over our kitchen, and we should thank Him for it. The complexity and chaos we are experiencing is meant to drive us back to dependence upon Him and shatter the false trust we've put in our system, structures, institutions.

The Lord is mischievously throwing dog food and waiting for our reaction. What will it be? Will you, like Joshua, fight to maintain your illusion of control? Or, will you accept that you don't have it and never will?

Complexity accelerates the mission of God.

The Lord had a reason for pouring out His Spirit on Medad and Eldad in the camp rather than at the tabernacle. Joshua saw it as a bad thing that must be stopped because it didn't follow the God-ordained plan. Moses, however, realized that the spread of God's presence among His people was always a good thing, even when it complicated simple systems, because ultimately it advances the mission of God.

We see this throughout the New Testament. In Acts 8, when persecution came upon the believers in Jerusalem and they were scattered, it complicated the church, but it also advanced the mission. In Acts 10, when Peter discovered that Gentiles were receiving the Spirit of God, it shattered his simple, God-ordained categories that said Jews were blessed and Gentiles were cursed. Gentiles' receiving God's Spirit complicated things, but it also advanced the mission. In Acts 15, when Paul and Barnabas had a strong disagreement over whether or not to take John Mark on their missionary journey and they split up, it complicated things, but it also advanced the mission.

> What we perceive as unexpected, complicated, and undesirable, God uses to leap His mission ahead at a pace that we never could.

We could trace this trend all the way through church history. What we perceive as unexpected, complicated, and undesirable, God uses to leap His mission ahead at a pace that we never could. So we need to be careful not to lament all complexity as bad, evil, or a scheme of the enemy. Instead, we must discern the difference between good complexity and bad complexity.

Bad complexity is like a Rube Goldberg machine. Those are the massive, jerry-rigged contraptions that fill an entire room with moving ropes, ramps, bowling balls, and buckets. One small motion, like a marble rolling or a domino tipping, begins a long and complicated chain reaction. The machines have been made popular recently on YouTube by OK Go, a pop rock band known for their quirky music videos. A Rube Goldberg machine is a huge, inflexible apparatus that accomplishes one simple task. It's not very useful, but it can be immensely entertaining.

Good complexity, in contrast, is like a Swiss Army knife—an elegant, nimble instrument that can accomplish an impressive number of tasks. No one would say Swiss Army knives are simple. They are intricate, with many precisely engineered parts, but this complexity of design paradoxically makes them adaptable and easy to use.

Many churches, and by extension many missions organizations, are marked by bad complexity. They are like Rube Goldberg machines—not very effective, but very entertaining to watch. They construct massive systems of control that are far larger than what is required for the task, and they are dangerously fragile. If one element of the system or environment changes, the weakness of the whole church or organization is exposed.

For example, Christmas predictably falls on a Sunday about every seven years, and every seven years many larger churches find themselves unable to hold worship services on that Sunday. Why? With more people staying home to open gifts with their families, these large churches cannot secure the hundreds of volunteers necessary to direct traffic, serve in the nursery, and run the other functions of the massive worship operation. In addition, the smaller offering collected on Christmas Sunday would not cover the expense of heat and electricity for the massive, mostly empty building. Megachurches are impressive, complicated operations, but even a predictable change, like Christmas falling on a Sunday reveals their fragility and inflexibility. That is bad complexity.

On the flip side, consider the complexity of the house-church movement we see in many developing countries and in parts of the world where Christians face persecution. It reveals a different kind of complexity. It often lacks centralized organization or leadership. It can appear chaotic or unfocused. I recall a conversation I had with a ministry leader in one such country. I asked him, "How many churches are meeting here?" He did not know. "How many pastors do you have?" Again, he did not know. And yet the church was growing at an amazing rate, and it was robust, able to flex and adjust as conditions changed or opportunities arose. That church was still complex, but it was a good complexity.

I'm not advocating for a certain church or organizational structure—that will depend on your environment and mission field—but I am advocating for a reexamination of your structures. As things become more complicated, are your systems fragile or robust? Are they rigid or flexible? Are you pursuing good complexity or bad complexity? The anti-institutional bias that dominates younger Americans provides an opportunity to honestly reassess the bad complexity that marks too many of our churches and organizations.

Rather than putting all of our resources into facilities, systems, and structures, which we may discover are Rube Goldberg machines, what if we allocated more resources for equipping people? Human beings are complex, but the good kind of complexity. Like Swiss Army knives, we are flexible, robust, and adaptable. And when people are equipped and filled with God's Spirit, the mission will advance in suprising ways.

Complexity uncovers our hidden motives.

When he was told about Eldad and Medad being filled with the Spirit and prophesying in the camp, Joshua was upset and told Moses to stop them. Moses, however, recognized the real source of Joshua's anger. "Are you jealous for my sake?" he asked Joshua.

Joshua, it seemed, saw Eldad and Medad's prophesying in the camp as a threat to Moses's reputation and authority. Remember, Moses had ordered the elders to assemble at the tabernacle to receive God's Spirit. Eldad and Medad had not followed Moses's command but received the Spirit and were prophesying nonetheless. This threatened to undermine the simple, linear authority structure established by God and diminish Moses's reputation among the people. The text is also mindful to include that Joshua had been Moses's assistant from his youth. In other words, Eldad and Medad were not just a threat to Moses's reputation, but to Joshua's as well.

> Rather than operate like the wind, we'd prefer the Spirit operate like an electric fan that we can control to perpetually blow in the same direction.

The complexity that God unleashed by acting outside the expected system revealed the motives of Joshua's heart. He wasn't primarily concerned with the advancement of God's work, but rather the protection of Moses's leadership, and by extension his own.

This is something we see in many legacy churches and organizations. God may have used a leader or institution in remarkable ways, but when the ministry encounters stagnation or decline due to unexpected complexities, they can begin to behave like Joshua. Rather than embracing a new movement of God, they become fixated on maintaining the old way of operating and may even express anger or outrage at those associated with the new approach.

In John 3, Jesus compares the Spirit to the unpredictability of the wind. "You do not know where it comes from or where it goes." Likewise, the Spirit can do amazing things through a leader and a ministry for many years, but if the Spirit shifts to blow in a new or unexpected direction, we may, like Joshua, resist this change. Rather than operate like the wind, we'd prefer the Spirit operate like an electric fan that we can control to perpetually blow in the same direction.

Moses reacts very differently, however. Unlike Joshua, he does not resist the new thing God is doing. He does not take offense that the Spirit operated outside the bounds of his authority or leadership. He is not primarily concerned with his own reputation or the perpetuation of his ministry. Instead, Moses sees the bigger picture. He recognizes that there is something far better and more important than his leadership structure or organization. Foreshadowing what would unfold on the day of Pentecost, Moses says, "Would that all the LORD's people were prophets, that the LORD would put his Spirit on them!"

Moses recognizes that control is not the goal—empowerment is! He does not want the people dependent upon him to encounter God or know His will. He wants every person to experience the Lord as personally and as intimately as he does.

There is no question that churches, denominations, and missions organizations are facing challenging times, but we have a calling higher than maintaining those institutions. We have a goal greater than keeping control of resources. The entire purpose of churches, denominations, and missions organizations is to empower God's people.

Is it possible that your stress is rooted, like Joshua's, in the fear that God is empowering His people outside the system you have created or been so long accustomed to? That isn't something to lament, and it certainly isn't something to resist. That is something to celebrate. The new complexities we are seeing should be a call for us to reexamine our own motives and goals.

Frank Zappa feared that the world would end through nostalgia. There is a spirit of nostalgia that is threatening the evangelical world today. As generations change and their values shift from the familiar ones that fueled evangelicalism over the last century, the temptation is to look backwards and cling to the way things used to be. The temptation is to be like Joshua and condemn the new, unexpected things complicating our lives and organizations and fight to keep our systems recognizable and under control. But in doing so, we may be impeding rather than advancing the movement of God in the world.

Instead, we must embrace this new complexity, because it shatters our illusion of control, it advances the mission of God, and it uncovers our hidden motives. This present complexity is not a curse. It is a blessing. We must pray for the grace to recognize it as such.

REFLECTION AND APPLICATION

Consider how God has metaphorically messed with your dog food in the past. What lessons did you learn from these unexpected complexities? How did they ultimately deepen your faith?

Is your ministry marked by bad complexity (the Rube Goldberg machine) or good complexity (a Swiss Army knife)? Discuss this with your leadership team.

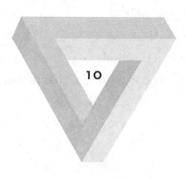

10

REDUNDANCY

I LIKE AIRPLANES. Given the amount I travel, it is good that I do. Watching these incredible aluminum and composite monuments of human ingenuity makes the atrocious environment of most American airports almost bearable. Modern airliners are among the most complicated machines ever built, with some containing over four million parts. But they are still regarded as the safest form of transportation.

There are over 20,000 commercial flights every day in the United States, and over 100,000 daily flights globally. If you were to drive rather than fly one of those routes, you would be 100 times more likely to be killed.[1] (Your chance of dying increases 3,000 times if you ride a motorcycle.) Perhaps more surprising, since 1980, the numbers of airplanes, flights, and passengers have doubled, but accidents per year have been declining. Flying is five times safer than it was thirty years ago.

How is that possible? There are many factors that contribute to air safety, but a significant one is what the industry calls "redundancy." Modern airliners are engineered so that everything necessary for flight has a backup—engines, control systems, computers, fuel lines, hydraulics, even the pilot. As a result, no single failure should cause an aircraft to crash.

The brilliance of redundancy was displayed in 2010 when an engine on a Qantas A380, the world's largest passenger jet, violently exploded in flight, sending shrapnel through the wing and fuselage. The accident report euphemistically called it an "uncontained engine failure."

The A380 was severely damaged. The engine was destroyed, numerous control systems had been severed by the flying debris, fuel was leaking, flaps on the left wing were inoperable, and the landing gear was damaged. Still, the pilots were able to fly for almost two hours before safely landing the aircraft.

Redundancy saved the day.

A century of powered flight, and a century of powered flight *accidents*, has led engineers to understand why planes crash. This knowledge has resulted in airliners designed to withstand almost any imaginable failure. By learning from past accidents, today's modern airliners are robust, or what author Nassim Nicholas Taleb would call "antifragile."[2]

This lesson from civil aviation may be relevant for the church today. Many churches, both large and small, seem to engineer their ministries around the antithesis of redundancy: singularity. They are dangerously fragile because a single leader is often the focus of nearly everything that happens, and not just on Sunday morning. I've seen some churches become paralyzed when the senior pastor is on vacation or even just out of the office. He is expected to provide guidance on every decision, every committee, every tiny detail of the church's life and ministry.

When it comes to the daily operations of an organization, many of us can recognize the dangers of singularity and say, as Jethro did to Moses, "What you are doing is not good" (Ex. 18:17). But what about the issue of singularity on a longer time horizon? For example, I recently watched a video of two pastors of larger churches discussing their succession plans. One shared how his church is establishing a redundancy of leadership so his retirement won't send the church into a tailspin. The church is actively engineering multiple congregations, multiple leaders, and multiple teachers to take the place of their founding pastor.

The other didn't yet have a plan. If his critical role in that ministry suddenly failed or became vacant, it would put the whole organization in jeopardy. Since recording the video, the church has apparently started a three-year transition to phase out the existing senior pastor and install a new leader. But will they simply replace him with another superstar preacher, or will they instead reengineer the ministry with greater redundancy?

The danger of fragility is increased by the recent trend toward video-based, multisite congregations. Rather than mitigating the risk of having a single teaching pastor, it actually compounds it by making more people in more congregations dependent upon one person. If that one pastor leaves or suffers an "uncontained failure," the impact will be far more devastating.

Whenever I've discussed the inherent fragility of video-based, multisite church structures, advocates will invariably mention the efficiency and effectiveness of this model. Who can disagree? Utilizing one highly gifted speaker to impact thousands of people in multiple cities is undeniably efficient. And trying to operate a multi-leader, multi-teacher, multi-congregation network is very complicated and expensive.

But when did efficiency and effectiveness become the highest values for ministry? Building airliners with multiple engines, fuel systems, computers, and flight controls is very complicated as all of those redundant parts add weight to the airplane. More weight results in burning more fuel to move through the air. Burning more fuel costs the airlines more money to operate the airplane. Those higher costs are transferred to passengers in the form of higher fares. It might be possible to build a very inexpensive airplane with only one engine, one pilot, and one computer, and to charge only $9.99 per passenger—but would you want to fly on it?

Engineering a ministry to be antifragile with redundancy is not efficient, but that shouldn't stop us from investigating its other benefits. Consider the story from The Next Level Church (TNL) that *Leadership Journal* published back in 2008.[3] TNL opted for a team-based leadership structure with no senior pastor, no superstar teacher, and no ministry singularity. In the interview they admit the inefficiencies of the model. But the redundancy also created stability.

At one point, one of TNL's pastors was facing a rough season in his marriage. The rest of the team decided the best way to care for him was to give him and his wife time away from the church to focus on healing. Dave Terpstra, one of TNL's other pastors at the time, said of this pastor, "If [he] had been the senior pastor, the church couldn't have handled the crisis. The entire church would have been handicapped by his inability to lead and shepherd during that season."

The redundancy built into the church's structure allowed both this pastor and the congregation to maintain stable flight. The pastor whose marriage was in crisis recalls the entire time as "really healthy." He was able to focus on his family, and the church didn't falter.

When pastors are confident that their church can function or even flourish without them for a season, they are more likely to find the courage to seek help for themselves or their marriages. As long as the entire system is built on the premise of singularity rather than redundancy, pastors will be incentivized to deny their needs and minimize their problems. The pastor cannot risk sharing a weakness or admitting a failure if there is no copilot to take the controls. Therefore what may have started as a manageable challenge is allowed to expand into an insurmountable disaster. In short, singularity may be more efficient in the short run, but redundancy keeps more leaders serving and churches thriving in the long run.

Maybe if the church learned a few lessons from the aviation industry, we wouldn't see so many pastors and congregations crashing and burning. With a great many Baby Boomer pastors nearing retirement, and their churches facing transitions, the risks may only be increasing. So many of these churches, especially the personality-driven megachurches, were engineered on singularity with one very dynamic leader/teacher at the center. How will they transition? How will they reengineer their ministries? Will singularity continue to be the fragile norm? Or will more congregations come to embrace the wisdom of blessed redundancy?

REFLECTION AND APPLICATION

Review your ministry structure with your leadership team. What are the most fragile points? Where would the failure of a single part inflict the most harm on the flock and their calling? Prayerfully consider how to respond to these areas of weakness.

If you could be absolutely certain that the ministry would thrive without your direct engagement, how would you structure your time differently? What areas of struggle would you feel more freedom to acknowledge and address?

11

BREVITY

THE MOST CELEBRATED speech in American history was
less than three minutes long. Lincoln's address at Gettysburg was only 269 words, but it captured the history, pain,
and aspirations of the nation with soaring eloquence and
inspiring imagery.

Many forget that Lincoln's speech was not the keynote
at the ceremony that day. The featured speaker was Ed-
ward Everett, a celebrity orator. His address at Gettysburg
was 13,607 words, over two hours long—not unusual for
a gifted speaker in the nineteenth century. After the event,
Everett wrote to the president saying, "I should be glad if I
could flatter myself that I came as near to the central idea
of the occasion, in two hours, as you did in two minutes."

As a preacher I have to remind myself that brevity can
be as effective as it is beautiful. I don't believe every sermon
should be as brief as the Gettysburg Address, but most of

mine would benefit from a nip and a tuck. Lincoln's famous speech makes me wonder if I might accomplish more by speaking less, and whether a great deal of what I cram into a message is more about meeting expectations (mine and the congregation's) than truly benefiting my hearers.

Sometimes I feel stretched by the service order that calls for a thirty-minute sermon. What if I only have twelve minutes of meaningful content to share? That's what the cute illustration about my six-year-old is for, and if that's still not enough, I can always read a lengthy C. S. Lewis quote or show a clip from the latest Christian(ish) movie. The structure of most evangelical worship services can force the pastor to stuff his sermon sausage with indistinguishable bits and pieces simply to fill the space between the enriched bun of sentimental music. Is it nutritional? Hey, McDonald's didn't reach "billions and billions" by serving health food.

> The error pastors make is assuming that Sunday sermons are primarily for teaching content rather than inspiring devotion.

More often, we face the inverse problem—we have too much to say and refuse to edit our remarks. In the last year, I've had to preach sermons on tough topics, including the doctrine of the Trinity, the incarnation, and Genesis 1. One could easily conduct a weeklong seminar on each of those topics and still not cover them sufficiently. For this reason, a preacher will take every minute he is allotted, and very often more, to squeeze in everything he can.

The error pastors make is assuming that Sunday sermons are primarily for teaching content rather than inspiring devotion. Teaching is critical, but a large-group lecture, as most of us experience on Sunday, is a terrible forum for effective learning. It's an ideal setting for preaching, however. Communicating the complexities of Trinitarian theology in fifteen minutes is impossible, but illuminating a vision of a loving God, who invites us to share in the perpetual, eternal relationship that exists between Father, Son, and Spirit? If a preacher can't accomplish that in fifteen minutes, he missed his true calling.

The difference between instruction and inspiration is what the crowd experienced in Gettysburg on November 19, 1863. Mr. Everett's two-hour lecture sought to educate the masses about the details of the war. He outlined the sins and conspiracies of the Confederacy and provided arguments for the Union's tactics. President Lincoln's far shorter address, on the other hand, didn't even contain the words "Union," "Confederate," or "slavery." Instead he lifted the sights of the audience to illuminate the ultimate meaning of the war and fill them with the hope that "this nation, under God, shall have a new birth of freedom."

Christians must learn the Bible—that is undeniable. Jesus commands us to make disciples, teaching them to obey all that He has commanded. It is the assumption that the Sunday sermon is the primary vehicle for this teaching, and that pastors should devote the largest amount of their time to sermon preparation every week, that we need to reexamine. Doing so, however, is not always welcomed by pastors, as I discovered years ago during my ordination process.

TRUE OR FALSE: A biblically faithful sermon can be preached in less than twenty minutes.

This question on my ordination exam caught me off guard. On a test designed to examine my theology, was sermon length really important? I quickly marked "True" and moved on.

A few months later I sat for my oral exam before a panel of luminary pastors. "On your written exam," the first questioner said, "you indicated that a biblically faithful sermon can be preached in less than twenty minutes."

"Yes, sir," I responded.

"Young man," he leaned over the conference table, "our culture is biblically illiterate. Even within the church most people cannot recite the books of the Bible or the Ten Commandments. Our greatest responsibility is to teach them God's Word. I spend at least thirty hours every week preparing my sermon, and when I enter the pulpit, I preach for no less than forty-five minutes, because our people need to know the Scriptures!"

I'm giving you just a sample of the pastor's remarks to me. He delivered them with the same force and flair he used in the pulpit—voice inflection, hand gestures, literal Bible pounding. He monologued like a James Bond villain, affording me precious time to calculate my response. Finally, after a dozen points and after the pastor felt his passion for the issue had been sufficiently communicated to everyone in attendance, he landed his question.

"So, how on earth can you justify only preaching a twenty minute sermon?"

"Well," I said, "when I thoughtfully and carefully read the Sermon on the Mount, it takes me about twenty minutes."

He gazed at me across the table. "Good answer," he said. "Next question."

The Grand Inquisitor's torrent of words had been deflected with the precision of a single sentence. Do not underestimate the effectiveness of brevity.

(In case you're wondering, this chapter is 971 words. I'm still learning.)

REFLECTION AND APPLICATION

Undertake a review of your last two or three sermons. Reread your notes/manuscripts or listen to the recorded message. Upon reflection, what could have been removed from the message? What was unnecessary or included simply to fill time or draw attention to yourself rather than the Lord? Consider these lessons as you compose your next sermon.

Commit to cutting 10 percent of the time allotted to the sermon. What can you do with this additional time in the worship gathering to help your congregation catch another glimpse of Christ and His kingdom?

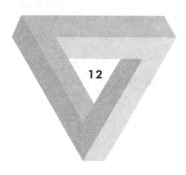

12

ILLUMINATION

FIFTEEN HUNDRED years ago, the emperor of Rome built a tomb for his beloved sister. The small building was designed in the shape of a cross with a vaulted ceiling covered with mosaics of swirling stars in an indigo sky. The focal point of the mosaic ceiling was an image of Jesus as a shepherd surrounded by sheep in a green paradise.

The Mausoleum of Galla Placidia still stands in Ravenna, Italy, and has been called by scholars "the earliest and best preserved of all mosaic monuments" and one of the "most artistically perfect."[1]

But visitors who have admired the mosaic in travel books and on postcards will be disappointed when they enter the mausoleum. The structure has only tiny windows, and what light does enter is usually blocked by a mass of tourists. The "most artistically perfect" mosaic monument, the inspiring vision of the Good Shepherd in a starry paradise, is hidden behind a veil of darkness.

But those who are patient, who endure the musty darkness and claustrophobia, will be rewarded. With no advanced notice, spotlights near the ceiling are turned on, illuminating the iridescent tiles of the mosaic, but only for a few seconds. One visitor describes the experience like this: "The lights come on. For a brief moment, the briefest of moments—the eye doesn't have time to take it all in, the eye casts about—the dull, hot darkness overhead becomes a starry sky, a dark-blue cupola with huge, shimmering stars that seem startlingly close. 'Ahhhhh!' comes the sound from below, and then the light goes out, and again there's darkness, darker even than before."[2]

The bright burst of illumination is repeated over and over again, divided by darkness of unpredictable lengths. Each time the lights come on, the visitors are given another glimpse of heaven, and their eye captures another element previously unseen—deer drinking from springs, garlands of fruit and leaves, Jesus gently reaching out to His sheep, who look lovingly on their Good Shepherd. After seeing the mosaic, one visitor wrote: "I have never seen anything so sublime in my life! Makes you want to cry!"[3]

We live in a dark world. Our hearts long for goodness, beauty, justice, and peace, but they are often hidden behind the shadow cast by evil and sin. This is why preaching is so necessary. Whenever the kingdom of God is proclaimed, it is like a bright burst of light. In those brief moments, the shadows recede and we are given a glimpse of a world behind the darkness. It is a sublime vision that reorders our perception of reality and leaves us hungry for more.

This understanding of preaching, the unveiling of an inspiring vision of God's kingdom, is not the one I've always held. I was formed to think that the primary purpose of preaching was instruction. This view expects the informed, articulate person behind the pulpit to teach the congregation divine truths and skills. The pupils are then expected to bury these seeds of biblical knowledge away in their brains, where in time they will germinate into godly values and behaviors, although few people seem surprised when they don't.

In Dallas Willard's VIM model of spiritual formation, he differentiates three parts:

Vision

Intention

Means

Instructional preaching falls under the third component—means. It teaches people the methods through which they can obey Christ. These "how to" sermons usually have clearly articulated, often alliterated, application points relevant to one's life.

I never questioned this "preaching as instruction" view until I stepped behind the pulpit myself. What I discovered disturbed me. Despite my hours of preparation, thoughtful use of visuals, and tangible takeaways, most people retained very little of the nutritious content offered to them. Like my lactose-intolerant son who spat up every ounce of milk we gave him as an infant, how would people thrive if they couldn't retain biblical knowledge? How would they grow? How would they follow the commands of Jesus?

What I have since discovered is that lecturing a passive audience for twenty to forty minutes, what one pastor has called "speaching,"[4] has been repeatedly proven to result in very low content retention. Likewise, adult education experts testify—along with a multitude of unregenerate pew sitters—that passive learning rarely transforms behaviors. Does this mean we should abandon instruction in the church? Of course not. After all, we are commissioned to teach people to obey everything Christ commanded. It simply means traditional preaching may not be the best medium for skill training and instruction.

But preaching is wonderfully designed for the prerequisite component of Willard's spiritual formation model, vision. Preaching this way will not always have the end goal of application, but rather inspiration. As Willard says, "It's the beauty of the kingdom that Jesus said was causing people to climb over each other just to get in."[5] Only after people have a vision of God (the love, beauty, justice, and power of His kingdom) will they be ready to intentionally seek and employ the means to experience him through obedience— an aspect of spiritual formation that occurs most effectively in smaller settings through the medium of relationship.

Preaching to inspire rather than instruct is a distinction we see in Jesus' own ministry. The Greek word for *preach* (*kerusso*) means "to announce." This is not the same as the word for *teach* (*didasko*), meaning "to instruct." In Mark's gospel we learn that Jesus came "preaching the gospel of God" and saying, "The time is fulfilled, and the kingdom of God is at hand." Jesus' preaching was a revelatory act. He announced the kingdom. He turned the lights on so people could see the kingdom that lay "at hand" just behind their present darkness.

Even Jesus' most celebrated sermon was intended more to inspire than instruct. The Sermon on the Mount paints a vivid image of a life lived within God's kingdom—a life that does not lust, lie, or manipulate; a life full of love, charity, and prayer. But the sermon includes very little "how to." Jesus' purpose is to reveal the kingdom, to illumine a sublime vision of a life in intimate communion with the Father.

Early in the gospel narratives, Jesus sends His new apostles out to proclaim the kingdom. Have you ever found that odd? These fishermen and tax collectors understood so little, and later chapters show the magnitude of their ignorance. Would you have put one of those guys in the pulpit?

But Jesus does not send them to "teach"—that command comes after His resurrection. Rather, He sends them to "preach." Teaching requires proficiency with a set of knowledge—knowledge these men did not yet possess. But preaching is different. Announcing the kingdom only requires one to have seen and experienced it. It's the difference between the barista announcing that my non-fat Earl Grey tea with one shot of sugar-free vanilla is ready (*kerusso*), and teaching me the chemical properties of solutions and the physics of heat that allowed the tea to brew (*didasko*).

Understanding the difference is crucial. If we see the purpose of preaching as primarily instructing, then it will be confined to an individual exercise, a responsibility granted only to the most biblically educated, articulate, and proficient in the congregation. But if we believe preaching is primarily the announcing of the kingdom, an unveiling of a vision of God's glorious reign and our life in it, then the responsibility to preach cannot lie solely with the pastor. It properly belongs with all of God's people—even ignorant fishermen.

Standing elbow-to-elbow with a herd of visitors in the Mausoleum of Galla Placidia is not a pleasant experience. In the darkness, odors become more acute. The ancient tomb smells, well, like an ancient tomb. Combined with the overly perfumed (and often sweaty) tourists, it creates a memorable olfactory experience. With neck craned, gazing into the darkness, one prays for the lights to come back on so the sense of sight can overpower smell in the brain's circuitry.

Teaching may be the domain of the spiritually mature, but preaching belongs to the whole body.

The more perceptive in the crowd will know when relief is imminent. Just prior to the lights coming on, a metallic "click" will resonate from the wall. Many Italian churches have a box along the wall for donations. But in the Mausoleum of Galla Placidia, the metal box offers an additional service. Inserting a coin will trigger the spotlights. This explains the unpredictable periods of darkness. The inspiring vision of heaven that everyone has endured darkness, odors, and one another to see is revealed only when someone in the crowd surrenders a donation.

If the purpose of preaching is illumination—the unveiling of a vision of God's kingdom—why do we limit that responsibility to only one person in the church? Why not allow others to drop their coins into the box for the encouragement and edification of the whole group? Surely a single mother, or recovering alcoholic, or teenager who has experienced God's reign can give us a glimpse of the kingdom as well. They, too, have coins to give. Teaching may be the domain of the spiritually mature, but preaching belongs to the whole body.

One way this happened in my church was a ten- or fifteen-minute segment of our Sunday gatherings we called "Offerings of Worship." People in the congregation are invited to stand and share a story, a prayer, a passage of Scripture, a song, or a piece of art—anything they wish to give as worship to God and encouragement to the community. The moments of silence can be awkward and uncomfortable, equivalent to the stretches of darkness in Galla Placidia's mausoleum (minus the odor). But then a coin is dropped, someone stands, and the lights burst on.

Kathy held back tears as she explained that both her mother and father are fighting cancer. Juggling her own young children and caring for her aging parents was one of the most difficult things she's ever faced. She shared about her father's profound faith in Christ. The peace and joy he exuded even during cancer treatments reminded her that Jesus is always with her and will never leave her. As Kathy sat down, Bill immediately arose. "Let's pray for our sister," he said. He led the congregation in blessing Kathy.

Michael, a nine-year-old in the second row, stood. He has a congenital disease that causes his bones to fracture easily and makes playing with other kids dangerous. "I'm new to the church," he said timidly. "I came with the Bradshaws; they're my neighbors. My family can be pretty difficult, and I just want to thank God for the Bradshaws. They've been really good to me." Michael showed everyone a picture he'd drawn of himself with the Bradshaw family.

Paul, a middle-aged professional, stood and shared about the addiction he's struggled with for decades—the darkness, despair, and guilt that plagued his soul. But the unwavering love of God, his wife, and other men in the church guided him to sobriety. He's not sure about the future, but each day he's learning to believe that God accepts him as His son.

Timothy, an immigrant from China, stood with his Bible open and began reading in Mandarin. No one in the congregation had a clue what he was saying. After a few minutes, he paused and began again. Through his heavily accented English, I was able to discern Psalm 1. When he finished, Timothy closed his Bible and his eyes and began singing a spirited Mandarin rendition of "Amazing Grace" with his arms lifted up. By the second stanza, the whole congregation was singing along in English.

Before I ever reached the platform that Sunday, the congregation had already seen glimpses of God's kindness to a struggling mother, His hospitality to a marginalized kid, His healing of an addict, and His grace that transcends culture and language. The veil of shadow that people experience all week had been pulled back, if only briefly, to reveal the beauty behind it. What more could I possibly add?

Like everyone else who had "preached" that morning, I stood from among the congregation—one more person with a coin to drop to reveal God's kingdom. I ascended the platform with a Bible to tell a story of God's work in ages past and to help the congregation see that same God at work today.

With this understanding, the sermon ceases to be the only glimpse of God's kingdom, or the single part of the service everything has been leading up to, and instead becomes one way among many that the darkness is dispelled and reality reordered.

I may have come more prepared than Kathy, Michael, Paul, or Timothy, and my content may have focused more on Scripture than personal experience, but my purpose was the same—to enrapture my brothers and sisters with the beauty of God and His kingdom, inspiring them toward faith and good works.

What they may not have known was that they had already encouraged me. Sunday morning is anything but worshipful for many pastors. We are so preoccupied with the details of the service that calming our souls and communing with Christ is nearly impossible. But hearing how others are encountering God, seeing His power in their lives, and catching a glimpse of His kingdom through their preaching has taught me to be a sheep again, and not just a shepherd.

The idea of opening the congregation to unrehearsed testimonies and sharing terrifies some pastors, and to be fair, I had my share of strange occurrences. Additionally, in very large churches, this kind of community expression is unworkable—one reason I still champion planting "accessibly sized" congregations. But there are other ways to move preaching away from an individual exercise and toward an expression of Christ's body.

During my years as a teaching pastor, we shifted the church steadily away from a single preacher and toward a team approach. Part of our motivation was practical. Having multiple congregations and wanting to develop new speakers was important, but a team approach had other hidden blessings.

I was sitting next to my wife on one of those rare Sundays when I had no official responsibilities. The associate pastor was preaching when Amanda leaned over to whisper something in my ear. "No offense," she said, "but I love it when Ron preaches."

"Why," I asked, "because you get to sit next to me?" I put my arm around her shoulder.

"No," she replied, rolling her eyes, "because when he preaches I really sense his passion for the lost." She was right. Ron spent most of his career as a missionary; he lives and breathes God's mission, and his heart aches for those who do not know Christ's love. I can preach faithfully about evangelism, but when Ron talks about it, there is an added power—the lights burn more brightly and illuminate that aspect of God's character more fully. Through him the body is inspired toward mission more effectively.

The New Testament tells us that Christ has given some to be apostles, prophets, evangelists, pastors, and teachers. And other passages highlight the diversity of gifts given for the edification of the whole body. But when only one person's gifts and personality are given expression in our gatherings, or if Sunday is seen as the private domain of teachers, we limit the vision of God His people experience.

Because many of us, both in leadership and in the pew, have been conditioned to equate ministry with preaching, any radical change to the pulpit ministry may prove impossible, or at least highly dangerous. Thankfully, pastors seeking to make their preaching an expression of the body can take several rudimentary steps in this direction.

John Ortberg encourages preachers to assemble a group from their congregation to function as a sermon preparation team. In this way, when the pastor stands on the platform to deliver the message, the sermon represents the work of a community of Christ's people and not merely one solitary voice.

Opportunities abound on the other side of the preaching event as well. Many churches have classes to discuss and apply the content of the sermon. The Internet, podcasts, social media, and blogs bring all kinds of possibilities. While I'm generally suspicious of employing technology in ministry, mostly because I see it done unreflectively, this is an exception. Some church websites allow the preaching pastor to interact with members on Sunday evenings about the morning's message. The conversation allows the congregation to contemplate responses and dig deeper into the ideas raised on Sunday morning.

A similar, although less technological, tool we used was called "Sermon 2 Small Group." Each week a small-group curriculum was created based on the vision presented in the sermon. Those who may not have felt prepared or confident enough to share in a worship gathering could express their experience of God in the more intimate setting of a home group. Groups were guided to discuss the vision presented in the sermon, share what they saw of God and His kingdom, and explore ways to apply that vision. During some seasons of the year, particularly Advent, Lent, and summer, similar guides were created for parents and children.

Like tourists standing in the mausoleum in Ravenna, many congregations may be unaware of the sublime beauty all around them. Preaching doesn't have to be merely instruction. We need to have the darkness of the world rolled away and a vision of God's kingdom illuminated before us. This responsibility to inspire does not lie with the pastor alone, but with all of God's people. If we welcome the body into the pulpit to drop their coins into the box and illuminate the kingdom for us all, the preacher and people alike may marvel at what is revealed.

What assumptions have shaped the preaching ministry of your community? What do you expect the sermon to accomplish? With other leaders, you honestly assess whether these expectations are being met and what changes to make in order to utilize the pulpit more faithfully.

Using Willard's VIM model of transformation, assess where each of the three components are occurring within your ministry community:

- Where are people receiving a ravishing vision of life with God?

- How are they being called to make an intentional decision to pursue this vision for themselves?

- Where are they being equipped and given the means to live out this vision?

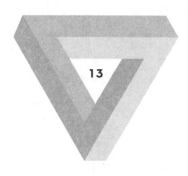

13

COMFORT

MY SIX-YEAR-OLD DAUGHTER is the most competitive personality in our home. While the other kindergarteners on her Tee Ball team are picking dandelions in the outfield, Lucy remains vigilant and "baseball ready" to make the play of the game. She recently came home from a summer backyard Bible camp disappointed. "The games were too easy," she insisted. "They need to make it harder to win."

Lucy's desire to be challenged reveals a fact often neglected in our culture—we only grow when we are uncomfortable, and too much comfort is not only unhelpful but can be downright dangerous. For example, a recent FAA study found that pilots are losing critical flying skills because they are underchallenged by state-of-the art planes that virtually fly themselves. Ironically, the push for safety through computer-automated flying is leading to more accidents as pilots "abdicate too much responsibility to automated systems."[1] That doesn't bode well for the introduction of self-driving cars in the near future.

I wonder if the same issue is present in the church. With the best of intentions, we have tried to make church gatherings a comfortable environment for both believers and seekers to learn about God. From the cushioned theater seats with built-in cup holders to the spoon fed, three-point sermon with fill-in-the-blank, pre-written notes, the only challenge most of us face on Sunday morning is actually getting our families to church. Once through the door, however, we can relax and switch on the autopilot.

If our goal is to teach people to obey all that Jesus commanded, then we may want to rethink our commitment to comfort on Sundays. Recent brain research has shown that when a person is comfortable, the more analytical functions of the brain necessary for learning remain disengaged. Psychologists refer to the brain as having a "system one" and a "system two."[2] System one is the more intuitive functioning that is active when relaxed, like when vegetating in front of a television or listening to a simple, clear sermon in a comfortable seat on Sunday morning.

System two is the analytical functioning of the brain that is required to rethink assumptions, challenge ideas, and construct new behaviors and beliefs. System two must be active to learn. Research shows that the brain shifts gears from system one to system two when it is forced to work, when it is challenged and uncomfortable.

For example, most people are able to concentrate better in settings with some background noise. The challenge of focusing on my friend's voice amid the clatter in the coffee shop shifts my brain from system one to two. By having to work to listen, I actually listen better than if we were to meet in the silence of my office. Of course there can also be too much background noise, making listening impossible, like at a NASCAR race or Chuck E. Cheese's. Think of it like riding a bike. Coasting downhill will never challenge your muscles or strengthen them. A steep incline will make riding impossible, also resulting in no muscle growth. The goal is to have just enough resistance to engage your muscles, but not too much.

These findings have made me rethink my tactics when preaching or teaching. I used to believe the best communication was crystal clear, simple, and easy to listen to. For this reason, like many other preachers, I was persuaded by advocates of PowerPoint and multimedia to use visual aids in order to make my communication easier. But is easier the right goal, or should we be seeking engagement, which requires more work of our listeners rather than less? I've largely stopped using slides or pre-written notes. If someone is going to "get" something from my sermon, I now want them to have to work for it—at least a little.

We can all agree that Jesus was a brilliant communicator, but when we study His methods, it is obvious that His audience's comfort was not a significant consideration. In fact, Jesus taught in a manner that engaged His listeners and challenged them. He expected them to work in order to understand His teaching. He asked them questions, wrapped His teaching in opaque parables, and often taught in distracting settings. Jesus was anything but crystal clear, simple, and easy to listen to. Even now, when we engage His teaching through the Gospels, it requires effort—and a large dose of grace—to understand Him. He never gave a three-point alliterated sermon, and neither did His apostles.

I'm certainly not opposed to clear communication, but our cultural drive for comfort and accessibility may have unintended side effects. All of us, just like pilots, drivers, and athletes, do not thrive by being underchallenged, but by turning off the autopilot and engaging in their own journey.

REFLECTION AND APPLICATION

How have you made church too "easy" for people? How have you set the bar too low? Discuss this with your leadership team and prayerfully consider where God is leading you to challenge people to take more responsibility for their own spiritual development.

Read the apostle Paul's description of his own communication ministry in 1 Corinthians 2:1–5. Being a highly trained Pharisee and familiar with Greek rhetoric, why did Paul decide not to display these desirable qualities in his preaching? What tools at your disposal might you intentionally not employ in your own preaching?

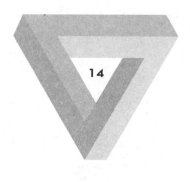

REST

"WHY DO WE work so hard?"

The question is asked by a man standing before a pool and manicured lawn. "Other countries, they work, they stroll home, they stop by the cafe, they take August off. Off. Why aren't you like that? Why aren't we like that? Because we're crazy, driven, hard-working believers, that's why."

The 2014 Cadillac commercial featuring this message was heavily criticized for endorsing materialism and workaholism, but what critics often overlooked was the ad's accuracy.

According to the International Labor Organization, Americans work more, take less vacation, and retire later than people in any other industrialized country.[1] By any measure work is an enormous, even overbearing, part of our lives. Our culture is more work-centered than any other on the planet. Given this reality, those of us committed to Jesus Christ cannot ignore work as a critical area of spiritual formation, but two-thirds of churched adults surveyed by Barna Group said they have not heard any teachings about work at their church.[2]

At a recent ministry event to address this topic, a few pastors challenged me. One asked, "Does the church really need to be talking more about work in a culture that's already obsessed with it?" That's a fair question, but let's apply the same logic to another cultural obsession—sex. For generations many churches avoided talking about sex apart from periodically condemning the culture's warped sexual values. By failing, decades ago, to offer a plausible alternative to the sexual idolatry of the culture, the church is now desperately seeking to regain its credibility on the subject. Thankfully, most pastors have abandoned this ignore-or-condemn approach to sex for a more mature, biblical discussion about this inescapable part of our humanity and spirituality.

I am concerned that we are repeating this error around our culture's vision of work. We are seeing the rise of a work-obsessed generation. While Millennials are generally underemployed and burdened with equal amounts of student debt and self-importance, a disproportionate number of them also believe they are destined to change the world and become famous in the process. More of them are also delaying marriage longer than previous generations in order to focus on their careers. This means more young adults are finding their identities through their work than through their families or faith.

Millennials are accepting our culture's message that their value is defined by their achievement, and that work

This perspective is predicated on a belief in the autonomous individual, that each person is free to choose how she wishes to live. Nothing external to the self—government, society, God, or even biology—should infringe on an individual's desires. This understanding of the self has led to a dramatic shift in the sexual vision of our culture, but these same values are also influencing our vision of work.

We assume that the work we do in the world is a matter of personal desire. We often ask children, "What do you want to do when you grow up?" By itself this is a harmless question, but behind it lurks a vision of individual autonomy with no room for God. We have abandoned the belief that any external agent should assign us our work. Our families, our communities, and even our God should not infringe on our individual professional desires. As with our sexuality, we have rejected the idea that our work is a calling we receive from outside of ourselves. We have rejected a theology of vocation.

Before the Reformation it was believed the word *vocation*, which comes from the Latin *vocare,* meaning "to call," only applied to the clergy. Based on their reading of Scripture, Luther, Calvin, and others rejected this limited view of vocation. Instead they insisted that God calls all Christians to their work. First, the Reformers said we are all called to unity with Christ. Second, all Christians share a set of common callings as revealed in the Scriptures. Third, we are each called to a specific, good, God-honoring work in the world. We all have a vocation.

But how do we discover our vocation? How do we know

is primarily about self-satisfaction rather than advancing the common good. In other words, the same values that fueled the sexual revolution experienced by their parents are now being applied to Millennials' vision of work, and once again the church is largely silent.

Ignoring work or condemning our culture's idolatry of it is not enough. Instead we have the challenging task of affirming the original goodness of work as a God-ordained part of our humanity without falling into the culture's trap of making work into an idol. We must cultivate a redeemed vision of work. In a culture full of "crazy hard-working believers," however, that is not easy. Just as a redeemed vision of sex requires affirming the importance of both desire and self-control, a redeemed vision of work requires both affirming our labor and resting from it.

A few years ago, my brother and sister-in-law took me to a concert at the Hollywood Bowl while I was visiting Southern California. As the sun was setting behind the outdoor amphitheater, the members of the orchestra began taking their seats. The sound of the musicians tuning their instruments was chaotic and unpleasant. Finally, the conductor emerged. He calmly raised his arms over his noisy orchestra. Silence. After a few moments of quiet anticipation, the conductor's hands moved and the music began.

While the musicians were tuning their instruments, they were making sound but not music. "Music," said composer Claude Debussy, "is the silence between the notes." It is the orderly rhythm of sound and silence that creates melodies and the soul-stirring music that lifts our spirits. Without silence, there is no music, only noise.

Similarly, redeeming work requires an orderly rhythm of work and rest. Without regular periods of rest, our work loses its meaning and value and deteriorates into chaotic toil. We may ridicule cultures that legislate six-hour work days and eight weeks of annual paid vacation, but ceaseless work does not lead to flourishing, either. What our culture has lost is a rhythm of work and rest in a frantic pursuit of achievement. We have become as work-saturated as we are sex-saturated, and "more" has not proven to be "better." We are making a lot of noise but very little music.

The most obvious example is the loss of the Sabbath. A weekly day of rest as prescribed by Scripture no longer fits with the demands of an ever-growing consumer economy, and even many Christians see it as an antiquated rule of life. But taking a day each week to rest is more than a way to find rejuvenation. Sabbath gives us the opportunity to step back from our immediate demands to put life into perspective, to appreciate the fruit of our labor, and to see our work in the larger context of God's work. In other words, far from diminishing the importance of work, Sabbath frames and defines our work so we can see its true value. Sabbath is when the Cosmic Conductor raises his arms to bring silence and stillness over His noisy orchestra so that something truly beautiful may be born.

There are more subtle ways we've lost a work/rest rhythm as well. Mobile technology means many of us never leave the office. Research has found that 84 percent of us check our phones before getting out of bed in the morning.[3]

Some of us are checking emails and responding to work issues all evening, during meals, and I'm guessing even during worship gatherings.

Advocates call it multitasking and say that technology allows us to work from anywhere. In truth it causes us to work everywhere. Clifford Nass, a psychology professor at Stanford University, says multitasking is a myth that wastes more time than it saves.[4] Just as the constant consumption of pornography will distort our ability to experience real intimacy, Nass says the evidence shows that constant engagement with digital technologies may be killing our concentration and creativity rather than cultivating them. In our drive to do more, we may accomplish less. The answer, says Nass, is more time for rest and reflection.

I have found that transforming the noise of toil into the music of work requires weekly and daily rhythms of rest. Keeping boundaries on my phone usage, pausing regularly through the day for prayer and Scripture reading, and practicing the Sabbath have not diminished the value of work in my life, but instead have helped me appreciate its value far more.

Our culture is not very good with boundaries. We frequently confuse license with liberty; we think that freedom is the absence of all restrictions. This is certainly true in our cultural attitude about sex. Previous generations passed laws regulating acceptable sexual behavior, defining marriage, limiting appropriate dress for women and men, and restricting reasons for divorce. Such laws are now seen as antiquated and even discriminatory.

what work God is calling us to? Unlike our common callings, which can be found by reading the Bible, I cannot open to a chapter and verse to discover my specific calling. Discerning our specific callings comes through a mature communion with the Holy Spirit. In other words, a theology of vocation is contingent upon a practical theology of prayer. But if we do not slow down, cease from our work, and learn to commune deeply with God, we will not be equipped to hear His call.

We see this pattern in Jesus' own communion with His Father. The beginning of His public ministry, the selection of His apostles, and His journey to the cross were all started after first ceasing from His work and devoting space for prayer to discern the Father's calling.

I regularly meet with college students who are eager to discuss vocation. "How do I know what I'm supposed to do with my life?" they sometimes ask me with more than a little anxiety depending on how close they are to graduation.

"Tell me about your communion with God," I'll ask.

Some have been confused by this question. They assume finding their vocation is a process of studying Scripture more carefully, exploring their gifts through an assessment, or uncovering a great need in the world they should devote their lives to remedying. Those are all well and good, but they also feed our culture's preference to take rather than receive. Without a robust communion with God through which we discern His call, we revert to the autonomous self. We think that our work in the world is determined by ourselves. We ask, "What do I want to do?" rather than,

"What is God calling me to do?" The former is predicated on personal preference or self-awareness, the latter on prayer and self-surrender.

The fruit of our work is not determined by how much we accomplish around us, but by how connected we are to God's Spirit within us.

Many of the callings that have shaped my life have been received in silence and solitude, including my call into ministry. These callings were subsequently affirmed by others in the church, but the process started by cultivating the space in my life for prayer and reflection.

Henri Nouwen noted that we like to stay busy because we want to avoid the noise within us. "Your inner life is like a banana tree filled with monkeys jumping up and down," he said.[5] The discipline of rest forces us to acknowledge and tame our inner monkeys. Only then can we hear God's calling, and with that clarity engage our exterior world accordingly. In this way the fruit of our work is not determined by how much we accomplish around us, but by how connected we are to God's Spirit within us.

If a redeemed vision of work in our workaholic culture means cultivating a rhythm of rest and the space to discern God's calling, then we need to ask what the church's role is in reestablishing these healthy patterns. Christ has called pastors to shepherd His sheep. That metaphor certainly includes feeding, leading, and protecting the flock of Christ, but we often overlook the shepherd's role in providing rest. "He makes me lie down in green pastures. . . . He restores my soul," says David of his Shepherd in Psalm 23.

When I left my full-time pastoral role some years ago, I began keeping track of my time in a journal. What I found surprised me. Between my work, my family relationships, the tasks of maintaining my home, yard, and fitness, I concluded that about 12 percent of my time was flexible. With this 12 percent I could read a book, volunteer at the homeless shelter, or take a nap. This 12 percent was also what the church was eager to fill.

It was often indirect and subtle, but from the moment I entered the church building on Sunday mornings, I felt like my 12 percent was being targeted. Whether it was the children's ministry seeking volunteers, or the upcoming missionary dinner, or the new tutoring initiative with the local elementary school, between the songs and sermon, the morning was crammed with ads. Sometimes they were even cleverly embedded in the sermon itself.

Ultimately it was my responsibility to say yes or no to these service opportunities, and I did not fault the church leaders for making me aware of the important work happening in our community. After all, I had preached for many years, pushing the very same activities with the very same good intentions. But after a few months in the pews rather than the pulpit, I felt exhausted. After a challenging week of work, there were some Sundays when attending a worship service brought more noise than music to my life. This led to me to reflect more honestly on my time on the pastoral team and how I had led the sheep entrusted to my care. Was I a shepherd who provided rest, or was I singularly focused on winning a larger slice of their 12 percent? In the most work-focused culture in history, was I helping to create a harmonious rhythm of work and rest or adding to the cacophony of noise and the idolatry of achievement?

I wonder if our culture's addiction to work, including within the church, is contributing to the church dropout rates. Based on conversations I've had with former church attenders, I think it is. Of course the work we're calling people to in the church is good, godly, and important, but when they've not been shown how to bring redemptive patterns of work and rest, activity and silence, into their professional lives, and when healthy rhythms of rest are also absent in the church's life, eventually the sheep will leave to find a pasture where they can lie down—even if it's a couch in front of a television on Sunday morning.

In 1974 Colonel William Pogue became the first American to go on strike in space. The astronaut was part of the last and longest manned mission aboard the Skylab space station. About halfway through the eighty-four-day mission, Colonel Pogue and the other astronauts requested ground controllers to adjust the work schedule for more rest. "We had been overscheduled," Pogue said. "We were just hustling the whole day. The work could be tiresome and tedious, though the view was spectacular."[6]

Ground control refused. The work was too important, they said, and time was limited. Some worried the astronauts' request was a sign of depression or a physical illness.

Pogue insisted neither was the case. They just wanted more time to look out the window and think, he said.

Eventually the disagreement between the crew and the controllers became so intense that the astronauts went on strike. Finally a compromise was reached that gave the crew more time to rest during the remaining six weeks of the flight. Pogue later wrote that having more time to look out the window at the sun and earth below also made him reflect more about himself, his crewmen, and their "human situation, instead of trying to operate like a machine."

Isn't Sunday supposed to be a time to cease from our work, gaze out the capsule window, and contemplate our lives and calling from a cosmic perspective? Aren't the songs, sacraments, and sermons supposed to reveal the wonder of God's kingdom amid the chaos of our world, and prepare us to reenter the atmosphere on Monday with a renewed sense of meaning? How did the goal on Sunday shift from feeding sheep to recruiting them?

There is no denying that our culture has embraced a broken vision of work. As the Cadillac commercial states, we are "crazy hard-working believers." But the church can help redeem work by modeling daily, weekly, and annual rhythms of rest. When we cease from labor, it affords us the space to discern God's calling so we may return to our work with a renewed focus. Rest also brings an order and efficiency to our work, as well as harmony to our lives. And when pastors shepherd their flocks on Sundays to see the world from a heavenly perspective, we may remember that the sheep are not machines, and neither are we.

REFLECTION AND APPLICATION

Talk with your leaders about what a daily, weekly, and annual rhythm of rest could look like within your ministry. How can you prevent the dehumanizing, mechanical drive of Church, Inc. from drawing you and your people away from a flourishing and abundant life in Christ?

How are you modeling a healthy life of work and rest? Because we see ourselves as doing "God's work," many ministers use this as an excuse for workaholism. What is deficient in your vision of God that causes you to skip the discipline of rest?

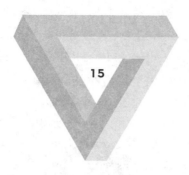

PLATFORM

I HAVE TO GIVE Stacy credit. It takes courage to speak directly to the pastor about a fault with his sermon. Most church members prefer to spread their disagreements peripherally around the congregation. Stacy chose the narrow way.

She was upset with a quotation I had used on Sunday. It came from a Christian author whom I had credited in my message. "He's a part of the emerging church," she said. "And the emerging church is heretical," she added with disdain.

"First of all," I asked, "did you disagree with the content of the quote I used?"

"No, I'm just upset that you would quote a heretic," she answered.

"Stacy, I can assure you the leader I quoted is not part of the emerging church. That term was made up by marketers who work for Christian publishers to package resources to younger pastors. The "emerging church" doesn't represent a single set of theological ideas. Besides, even if the leader I quoted was part of the emerging church, not everyone associated with it is automatically a heretic."

"Sure they are," Stacy insisted. "Chuck Colson said so, and he's on the radio." The words "and you're not" were absent from the end of her sentence but present in her tone. I didn't bother challenging her interpretation of Colson's broadcast, which I suspected she misunderstood, nor did I defend the reputation of the author I had quoted. I knew the battle was lost. I had been outmuscled.

The fact was Chuck Colson had more authority in Stacy's life and faith than I did. What authority I possessed had been built through years of shared community, sound teaching, and the vetting of denominational leaders. But it was no match for the authority Mr. Colson was granted in Stacy's life the first moment she heard him on the radio.

In marketing lingo, it's called *platform*. The logic is simple: the magnitude of your platform determines the weight of your authority. Someone with an audience of one million has more authority than a person with an audience of one hundred. The assumption we make, and this is where the trouble comes, is that a larger platform is a result of the person's competency, intelligence, or character. In the past this may have been the case (although I doubt it). Generally, large platforms were granted to those who had proven their authority. Today authority is granted to those who have simply proven they can build a platform.

Consider Oprah Winfrey. I have no doubt she is very competent when it comes to the media business, but I'm guessing the Queen of Talk is a lot less savvy about digital cameras. Still, when she featured a new Nikon on her "Favorite Things" show and called it "one sexy camera," it started to fly off store shelves. Why? Platform. Millions of people listen to Oprah, so she must be right . . . even about a digital camera.

How does this platform principle relate to pastoral ministry? Authority is best established through proximity—being in close personal contact so that trust can be established and grown. Marriage works this way. A man and woman in proximity over time (a.k.a. dating) develop enough trust to make a lifelong commitment to love and trust each other (a.k.a. marriage). This is what Paul had in mind when he told Timothy to choose leaders who are respected by all, and who have proven their faithfulness over time (1 Tim. 3:1–7). Authority is predicated upon a personal knowledge of those whom we submit to.

But when authority cannot be granted on the basis of proximity—actually knowing a person—we may grant it on the basis of popularity. In such cases we do not allow a person authority based on a track record of faithfulness, but based on the magnitude of their platform. I may not personally know Oprah, but surely millions of people can't be wrong.

Sadly, as our culture's capacity to engage and maintain meaningful relationships has deteriorated, we have seen a rise in popularity-based rather than proximity-based authority.

And the same trend is evident within the church. Just because someone has a large ministry or has sold millions of books doesn't mean we should automatically grant him authority over our life, faith, or congregation. As many entertainers, politicians, and church leaders have proven, it is possible to build a large platform and yet lack the character or competency to faithfully wield it.

Still, we foolishly think that by gaining more Twitter followers, Facebook friends, church attenders, or podcast subscribers we can prove our value and gain more authority. And we may be right, but it will be a shallow authority based on the size of our platform rather than the truth of our message, content of our character, or gravity of our soul. In the process we will miss the opportunity to establish the more hardy and biblical kind of authority that comes when we spend our time in close proximity with those we are called to lead.

> The antidote to popularity-based authority is the quiet power of pastoral presence.

This is where I had failed with Stacy. In my time at the church, I had had very little personal contact with her or her family. Because my proximity had not established much authority in Stacy's life, popularity entered to fill the vacuum. The solution is not to strive for a platform as large as the late Mr. Colson's by getting on the radio or selling more books in order to prove myself his equal. The antidote to popularity-based authority is the quiet power of pastoral presence.

Do your sheep actually know their shepherd? If you're like me, you may feel most at ease when alone, with a book, or in the task of studying and writing. However, ministry requires us to know and engage those we seek to shepherd. Consider how you can make yourself more available and relatable to those entrusted to your care.

Who is exercising influence in your ministry that has no constituted authority to do so? Are there media voices, radio personalities, or others your people are following? These may be godly, helpful leaders, but they may also be wolves in sheep's clothing. You cannot prevent people from engaging with voices outside your ministry, but what can you to do warn your flock of the dangers?

16

CELEBRITY

CELEBRITY PASTORS are not a new phenomenon, nor is our human tendency to exalt our leaders to unsustainable heights. What is new is the number of celebrity pastors and the speed with which they are being created and corrupted. Every generation has had a handful of well-known pastors, but why are there now so many, and how do they achieve so much influence with so little accountability? What explains the creation of an entire celebrity class within American evangelicalism?

There is more than a spiritual or psychological reason behind the rise of today's pastoral pantheon. There is a systemic economic force at work as well, what I call the "Evangelical Industrial Complex" (EIC).

First a little background. In 1961, in his farewell address to the nation, President Eisenhower warned about the unintended effects of the "military industrial complex." During

World War II, the massive industrial capacity of the United States was redirected to supply the weaponry necessary to defeat Nazi Germany and Imperial Japan. After the war, many factories returned to assembling Buicks and bicycles, but not all of them. For the first time, the United States had a permanent arms industry that relied on military conflicts for profit. Without war these corporations would collapse. Eisenhower, the celebrated army general who led the Allied forces to victory in Europe during WWII, worried that the industries created to end that war would now push the country to start many more. Many now consider Eisenhower's warning prophetic, given the exponential growth in military spending and wars over the last sixty years.

So, what do Eisenhower and the military have to do with the rise and fall of celebrity pastors? Well, just as America's militarism for the last seventy years is partially the result of systemic economic forces, so is the rise of the present clergy celebrity class. There is an Evangelical Industrial Complex that helps create and relies on celebrity leaders. Have you ever wondered why you don't see pastors from small or medium sized churches on the main stage at big conferences, or why most of the bestselling Christian authors are megachurch leaders?

Here's the answer we like to believe: The most godly, intelligent, and gifted leaders naturally attract large followings, so they will naturally have large churches, and their ideas are so great and their writing so sharp that publishers pick their book proposals, and the books strike a chord with so many people that they organically become bestsellers, and these leaders become the obvious voices to speak at the biggest conferences. As a result, they ascend to celebrity status.

Is this possible? Yes. Does it happen? Sometimes. Is it the norm? No.

Beyond the dubious ethics exhibited by some pastors in pursuit of fame, this market-driven cycle of megachurches, conferences, and publishers results in an echo chamber where the same voices, espousing the same values, create an atmosphere where ministry success becomes defined as mere audience aggregation. For example, some years ago I attended a ministry conference in a large arena. The glittering stage—as likely to host a gyrating boy band as a modern American pastor—was occupied by a solitary figure who had recently ascended the Olympian cliffs to join the pantheon of celebrity pastors. The young man began his address by noting how three years earlier he had attended the same conference with a seat in the "nosebleed section," but now he was speaking on the main stage (with a book to plug, of course). What had transported him from the periphery to the platform? He was not shy about admitting that his status had been elevated by the exponential growth of his church.

As he reveled in the glory of applause, I wondered how the pastors seated around me in the nosebleed section of the arena felt. Why had God chosen his church for rapid growth and not theirs? Why had he been plucked from obscurity and not them? And how were their definitions of ministry success being formed, or malformed, by this setting that celebrated the magnitude of a leader's audience rather than his maturity or wisdom, neither of which our young keynote speaker exhibited?

The real danger of the Evangelical Industrial Complex is not the elevation of immature and unaccountable leaders, but how these leaders in turn warp the vision of ministry held by the rest of us. They cause us to judge ourselves, our callings, and our ministries by a wholly unholy standard. Maybe that is why a growing number of us feel worse about our calling to ministry after attending ministry conferences, rather than better.

Where are the ministry conferences that celebrate those called to the house-church movement? Where are the brilliant, godly, wise, fifty-five-year-old pastors with gifts of communication, carrying timely messages and leading churches of two hundred? I meet such shepherds frequently, but never in the green room behind the main stage of a ministry conference. Such leaders would offer a very different vision of ministry success, one that would bring strength and healing to a burdened audience of pastors, but their voices do not serve the market demands of the EIC and therefore remain unaffirmed.

The Evangelical Industrial Complex is not maliciously seeking to suppress these alternative voices. Instead, their decisions regarding which voices to magnify are made by the cold, calculating demands of the market. Leaders within the EIC, however, often fail to recognize how their dispassionate business decisions and need for sustainable revenues also shape the evangelical movement and the spiritual lives of millions of people. For example, I spoke with a large ministry conference organizer about how speakers are chosen for the event. He confided that little if any attention is paid to a leader's teaching or doctrine. Instead, the conference requires "marquee" names that can sell tickets. As a result, I've attended a fair number of conferences where the teaching from the main stage has been atrociously unorthodox, but always passionate and entertaining.

In other church traditions there are ecclesiastical authorities who serve as gatekeepers. They guard pulpits and platforms to ensure only leaders who have been tested and approved are granted access to positions of wide influence. They take seriously the apostle Paul's instruction to appoint only mature leaders, not recent converts, with good character and a gentle spirit (1 Tim. 3:1–7). Within American evangelicalism, however, with its low ecclesiology and nondenominational bias, there are no bishops. There are no overseers to guard the flock from the influence and abuse of ungodly leaders filling our media, bookshelves, and conferences. In the place of a church hierarchy, we've built the Evangelical Industrial Complex; we expect publishers, conference directors, and radio producers to protect the flock from wolves. We trust them to filter out the immature, ungodly leaders, and for many years the managers of the EIC were willing to serve this function.

Those days are over.

> In the place of a church hierarchy, we've built the Evangelical Industrial Complex; we expect publishers, conference directors, and radio producers to protect the flock from wolves.

Chaos in the publishing world brought on by the immediacy of digital communication has put incredible pressure on the EIC to sell books and fill conferences profitably. Facing this existential threat to their businesses, managers within the Evangelical Industrial Complex are remembering that they were not appointed to shepherd us, but to sell to us. Those who had functioned as evangelicalism's bishops for decades have taken off their vestments to reveal the business suits underneath. That's not to say there aren't people working in Christian media who practice discernment and care about the character of the leaders they platform. There are. But industry-wide too often it's market demands, rather than biblical standards, that end up driving decisions.

The rise and fall of any celebrity pastor is merely a symptom of an underlying malady within American evangelicalism. Why are there now so many celebrity pastors? Because they generate a lot of revenue for the Evangelical Industrial Complex. Why do these pastors fall with such regularity? Because the Evangelical Industrial Complex uses a business standard rather than a biblical standard when deciding which leaders to promote.

REFLECTION AND APPLICATION

Consider withdrawing your support of operations within the EIC that platform or publish leaders who clearly do not exhibit godly character, biblical wisdom, or orthodox teaching. This is not a call to judgment, but to discernment.

Affirm and reward those publishers, radio programs, or conferences that do show wise discernment. Contact editors and program directors and ask them, "How do you decide who to publish or which leaders to feature at your event? What kind of accountability do you expect leaders to have in their ministries before you will platform them? Do you ask for character references before agreeing to give a leader a national audience?" If you are going to trust these businesses with the authority to choose what teaching and leaders influence your faith and leadership, maybe you should investigate how they make these decisions.

Return some of the authority you've granted to the Evangelical Industrial Complex to your local ministry authority. No matter how seriously the EIC takes its responsibility to protect the flock, we will never know the leaders we permit to shape our lives via books, podcasts, websites, and conferences. We need incarnate men and women to function in our communities as spiritual fathers and mothers. In the context of a relationship rooted in trust and love, we should allow them to speak into our lives with an authority that is earned and with a gravity that comes from the presence of Christ in their souls. This is what leadership in the church is supposed to be, and what the Evangelical Industrial Complex can never replace.

17

BOOKS

That's a common question among bookish pastors. Sometimes I hear it phrased, "Who do you read?" which is, among ministers, akin to dogs smelling each other's hind quarters. We're trying to determine one another's theological scent and whether we are among friendly or rival packs.

However, in most cases the question, "Who do you read?" is asked without malice. Pastors are simply looking for reading recommendations that will encourage their souls or sharpen their skills. When people ask me, my answer usually surprises them: "I read dead people."

What do I mean? In my previous role editing a Christian magazine, I received dozens of books every week from publishers. They were looking for some good press, an endorsement, or a review in our pages. Although some remarkable new books did cross my desk, most were immediately forgettable or cringe-inducing drivel. (Yes, I recognize the irony that at this very moment I am writing another book to add to the pile.) After years of exposure to this parade of publications, I decided to turn my attention away from what's new and toward what's timeless.

I figured that if someone has been dead for a while and his or her book is still in print and widely read, then it's probably worth reading. And, if we're honest, there are precious few books written by Christian authors today that will still be read in 24 months, let alone 24 years. (You may be holding one right now.) I want to use my reading time to immerse myself in powerfully formative material, and not just flash-in-the-pan trends by the latest pop-star pastor. Does that mean I never read living authors? Of course not. But if they're not dead, I'd like them to be pretty close (myself excluded). I can usually trust that an author looking down the barrel of eternity is not going to waste what time he has left on this earth writing bloated sentimentalities or mere ministry mechanics.

A few years ago my "read dead people" axiom was affirmed when Bill Hybels conducted an interview with Steve Sample, president of USC and author of *The Contrarian's Guide to Leadership*. Hybels, who is a voracious reader, was surprised to learn that Sample recommends reading less and not more. Here's an excerpt from their conversation:

> Hybels: One part of this book made me laugh out loud, because these are some of the strangest views I've ever heard—about what leaders should be reading. Tell us your theory.

Sample: My theory is that, to a greater extent than most of us realize, we are what we read. I think it was Thoreau who made the observation that reading one book necessarily precludes your reading hundreds of others. You have to make hard choices with respect to reading.

If you're in a leadership position, the least important things for you to read are newspapers and trade magazines and the like. Thomas Jefferson once said, "The man who reads nothing at all is better informed than the man who reads nothing but newspapers."

I allow myself ten minutes to scan *The Los Angeles Times* and *The Wall Street Journal,* and that's enough. But the other twenty minutes has to go toward reading substantive material.

Hybels: I've been telling leaders this for a long time: read everything you can read about leadership. You took my counsel one step further. You said, "Don't read just anything about leadership; read the 'supertexts' about leadership." What are you talking about?

Sample: Of the hundreds of thousands of things that men and women have written four hundred years ago or before, only about twenty-five to fifty are widely read today. So there's something very special about these twenty-five to fifty texts. They influence everything that is written and spoken in our society to an unprecedented degree.

You can usefully spend your time reading any of the supertexts, even over and over again, because they probably tell us more about human nature than anything else we have at our disposal. But for books that are not the supertexts, I think a person has to be very, very selective.

Amen! Allow me to mention a few of my favorite supertexts and dead people. I'm obligated to say C. S. Lewis (you know, for credibility), but in the area of contemplative reading and spiritual formation I also appreciate Thomas Kelly, Henri Nouwen, Teresa of Avila, Brother Lawrence, A. W. Tozer, and Thomas à Kempis. It's difficult to find better theological reflections than those of Calvin, Barth, or Augustine, regardless of whether your theology always conforms to theirs. I am also indebted to Xavier Loyola for the expansive spirituality he bestowed on the Jesuit tradition. Every pastor should also read Eugene Peterson (from the Not Dead Yet category) and Dallas Willard (from the Recently Departed category).

We shouldn't underestimate the influence a book can have on our lives or the direction of our ministry. I was given a book as a college freshman by a graduate assistant in the philosophy department that forever changed my view of faith. I was studying at a large state university, and my young Christian faith was preoccupied with reason, apologetics, and philosophy. The graduate assistant had been impressed with my work and must have deduced that I was a fledgling Christian—an exceedingly rare species in the philosophy department—and sensed the danger of malformation by my relentless focus on reason and argument. He handed me a small work by Henri Nouwen. Through that Dutch priest's pen, I began to see a previously invisible dimension of faith that required self-awareness and not just doctrinal knowledge.

For the last twenty-five years, Nouwen has been a constant companion of mine. His writings have helped my faith and influenced my work in countless ways, but because of his European, academic, and Roman Catholic pedigree, I probably would not have encountered him naturally through my teenage evangelical community. Nouwen's wisdom helped me avoid a number of pitfalls early in ministry and served as a counterbalance to the gravitational pull of Church, Inc. throughout my college and seminary training. I am a different Christian now because of his books and many others I've encountered.

Charlie "Tremendous" Jones is fond of saying, "Five years from today, you will be the same person that you are today except for the books you read and the people you meet." Therefore, choose your books, like your friends, carefully.

How do you curate your library? How do you determine what books to spend your time reading? Are you simply responding to popularity or the marketing tactics of those pushing the values of Church, Inc.?

Make a commitment with your leadership team to read a "supertext" together. (Something other than the Bible.) Discuss what the book reveals about human nature, God, and life, and how it all relates to your calling as ministers.

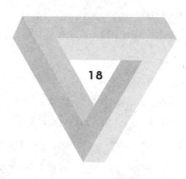

CONSUMERS

I DON'T DRINK COFFEE, but that didn't stop me from using the Starbucks across the street from my church as a second office. I prefer to sip my overpriced beverages in the armchair near the bay window. On this afternoon, I was meeting Greg and Margaret, members of our church I'd worked closely with for the last few years.

"We've decided to leave the church," Greg started. "For two months we've been church shopping." *Church shopping*—where did that dastardly term come from? I thought while gazing out the window at the swarm of suburbanites fluttering between The Gap, Banana Republic, Barnes & Noble, and Williams Sonoma.

"We really love the church," Margaret added to soften the blow. "It's been a great church for our family with a wonderful children's program, but our kids are teenagers now, and they prefer the music at Faith Community." I took a sip of my preferred drink—a tall, no whip, Tazo chai latte. Maybe I should have gotten the low cal, nonfat, grande Earl Grey.

Margaret continued, "Faith Community has so much to offer our family, and I think it's really important to go someplace the boys like. When your kids are teenagers, you'll understand." Having played her trump card (the kids), Margaret sat back in her chair believing no further discussion was necessary.

"What are you going to do when your kids leave home in a few years?" I asked.

"I'm not sure," said Greg. "Maybe we'll come back to the church."

"I hope you don't," I replied, meaning no malice. I did, however, relish the stunned look on their faces, if just for a moment. "I hope that you commit yourselves so fully to Faith Community—building strong relationships, serving with your gifts, participating in its mission—that you could never see yourselves leaving that church. I really believe God grows us most when we are committed to a community."

For the next hour we had a difficult but edifying conversation about their decision to leave. At the end of our time, I prayed for Greg and Margaret, and watched from my chair by the window as they drove away in their SUV with a chrome fish on the tailgate.

Every pastor has a story like that. Some of us have far more than we'd like to admit. It is the price we must pay for answering a call into ministry in a consumer culture.

Christian critiques of consumerism usually focus on the

danger of idolatry, the temptation to make material goods the center of life rather than God. However, this misses the real power consumerism carries. My concern is not materialism, strictly speaking, or even the consumption of goods—as contingent beings we must consume resources to survive. The problem is not consuming to live, but rather living to consume.

We now find ourselves in a culture that defines our relationships and actions primarily through a matrix of consumption. As the philosopher Baudrillard explains, consumption is a system of meaning.[1] We assign value to ourselves and others based on the goods we purchase. Your identity is constructed by the clothes you wear, the vehicle you drive, and the music on your iPhone. In short, you are what you consume.

This explains why shopping is now the number one leisure activity in America.[2] It occupies a role in society that once belonged only to religion—the power to give meaning and construct identity. As Pete Ward correctly concludes, "[Consumerism] represents an alternative source of meaning to the traditional Christian gospel."[3] No longer merely an economic mentality, consumerism has become the American worldview—the framework through which we interpret everything else, including God, the gospel, and church.

When we approach Christianity as consumers rather than seeing it as a comprehensive way of life, an interpretive set of beliefs and values, Christianity becomes just one more brand I consume, along with Gap, Apple, and Starbucks, to express my identity. And the demotion of Jesus Christ from Lord to label means to live as a Christian no longer carries an expectation of obedience and good works, but rather the perpetual consumption of Christian merchandise and experiences—music, books, T-shirts, conferences, and jewelry.

Approaching Christianity as a brand (rather than a worldview) explains why the majority of people who identify themselves as born-again Christians live no differently than other Americans. According to research from the Barna Group, most churchgoers have not adopted a biblical worldview; they have simply added a Jesus fish onto the bumper of their unregenerate consumer identities. As Mark Riddle observed, "Conversion in the US seems to mean we've exchanged some of our shopping at Wal-Mart . . . for the Christian Bookstore down the street. We've taken our lack of purchasing control to God's store, where we buy our office supplies in Jesus' name."[4]

During my conversation with Greg and Margaret at Starbucks, I asked them how they came to choose Faith Community as their new church:

Did you pray as a family about this decision? "No." Did you involve your small group or seek the wisdom of an elder in the decision? "No." Did you investigate the church's doctrine, history, or philosophy of ministry? "No." Did you base your decision on anything other than what you "liked"? "No."

How then do we make sense of their decision? Being fully formed in a consumer worldview, Greg and Margaret intuitively accept that the fulfillment of personal desire is the highest good. As a result, they chose the church that best satisfied their family's desires without bothering to consult their community, the Bible, or the Holy Spirit to determine the legitimacy of those desires. After all, in consumerism, a desire is never illegitimate; it is only unmet.

It's important to realize that people have not always lived this way. Consumers, like the goods they buy, were made and not born. The advent of mass production during the Industrial Revolution created previously unimaginable quantities of goods—far more than the market needed. Manufacturers suddenly needed a way to artificially increase demand for their products. Advertising was born.

Ads became the prophets of capitalism, turning the hearts of the people toward the goods they didn't know they needed. They subtly or overtly promised more comfort, status, success, happiness, and even sex to people who purchased their wares. In 1897 one newspaper reader said that in the past we "skipped [ads] unless some want compelled us to read, while now we read to find out what we really want."

Today, according to *The New York Times*, each American is exposed to 3,500 desire-inducing advertisements every day, promising us that satisfaction is just one click or purchase away. Rodney Clapp says, "The consumer is schooled in insatiability. He or she is never to be satisfied—at least not for long. The consumer is tutored that people basically consist of unmet needs that can be appeased by commodified goods and experiences."[6]

This constant manufacturing of desires has created a

culture of overindulgence. Obesity, sexual promiscuity, and skyrocketing credit-card debt are just a few signs. Although lack of self-control has always plagued humanity, for the first time in history, an economic system has been created that relies on it. An economist in 1955 said, "Our enormously productive economy . . . demands that we make consumption our way of life, that we convert the buying and use of goods into rituals, that we seek our spiritual satisfaction, and our ego satisfaction, in consumption."[7]

Our consumer economy has reached a point that if people began suppressing their desires and consuming only what they needed, our civilization would collapse. To prevent this, the satisfaction of personal desires has become sacrosanct. For example, during World War II, the government severely restricted public consumption of certain goods needed for the war effort. Following 9/11, however, Americans were repeatedly told that making any sacrifices to our indulgent lifestyles was tantamount to "letting the terrorists win." Under consumerism, the fulfillment of desire has become the highest good and final arbiter when making decisions—even when deciding where to worship.

It isn't difficult to see the incompatibility of this basic virtue of consumerism with traditional Christianity. Scripture champions contentment and self-control, not the endless pursuit of personal desires. Unfortunately, teaching and modeling these increasingly un-American values is not a high priority for Church, Inc. In fact, many churches are using the same desire-inducing marketing techniques pioneered by consumerism to draw people through their doors.

This should remind us that pastors and church leaders, me included, have also been greatly influenced by consumerism. Roger Finke and Rodney Stark, coauthors of *The Churching of America, 1776–1990*, argue that ministry in the United States is modeled primarily on capitalism, with pastors functioning as a church's sales force, and evangelism as its marketing strategy. Our indoctrination into this economic view of ministry may prevent us from recognizing how unprecedented it is within Christian history.

According to Finke and Stark, the American church adopted a consumer-driven model because the First Amendment prohibited state-sanctioned religion. Therefore, faith, like the buying of material goods, became a matter of personal choice. And, "where religious affiliation is a matter of choice, religious organizations must compete for members and . . . the 'invisible hand' of the marketplace is as unforgiving of ineffective religious firms as it is of their commercial counterparts."[8]

This explains why corporate models, marketing strategies, and secular business values are pervasive in American ministry—we are in competition with other churches for survival. We must convince a sustainable segment of the religious marketplace that our church is "relevant," "comfortable," or "exciting." And we must differentiate our church by providing more of the features and services people want. After all, in a consumer culture, the customer, not Christ, is king.

> In a consumer culture, the customer, not Christ, is king.

When I arrived at Starbucks to meet with Greg and Margaret, I first went to the counter to order a drink. The relatively simple menu on the wall is deceptive. There was a time when ordering coffee meant regular or decaf, cream or sugar. Today, Starbucks provides literally eighty-seven thousand beverage permutations. (Although the number is much smaller for those of us who consume tea rather than coffee to express our identity.)

While enjoying our drinks of choice, Greg and Margaret proceeded to explain how Faith Community Church had multiple services on Saturday and Sunday so they could choose to worship at a time that fit their busy schedule. My church only had three services at the time, all on Sunday morning. The youth group had multiple worship teams for their son, a drummer, to play on. Our student ministry only has one worship team. And, because Faith Community was "way bigger" than our church, it had more to offer Greg and Margaret, too. Ironically, they had come to our congregation years earlier from a smaller church. What goes around comes around.

One of the core values of consumerism is choice. With each additional option, the shopper is better equipped to construct their unique identity. Customization, creating a product that conforms to my particular desires, has driven businesses to offer an ever-increasing number of choices to consumers. Nothing represents this trend better than the shift from CDs to digitally downloadable music. Listeners don't have to buy an entire album to enjoy just one song. They now have instant access to millions of songs, and they can download them individually to create a personalized playlist. The demand for more choices has also driven the modern megachurch phenomenon. Although very large churches exist in other cultures, the American megachurch is unique in the world. Unlike those in Asia or Latin America, which are primarily networks of house churches, American megachurches are huge edifices designed with theaters/worship auditoriums, food courts/fellowship halls, and education wings/amusement parks. The goal is to provide religious consumers with as many choices as possible.

For example, some churches have embraced a digital variation of the "multisite" model with what the ministry industry now calls "video venues." Upon entering the church on Sunday, each family member can choose the worship setting that fits his or her personal desire. Simultaneously, grandma can sing hymns in the traditional service, mom and dad can enjoy coffee and bagels in the worship cafe, and the teenagers can lose their hearing in the rock venue. The value of family and congregational unity is drowned out by consumerism's mantra of individual choice.

"The inspiration for what this church is doing," reports one journalist, "comes from a place where freedom of choice and variety are celebrated: the American shopping mall." To which one video venue pastor responded, "I am very comfortable with a consumer mindset and use that as a tool to help reach people."[9]

Whether we're ordering a latte, downloading music, or worshiping God, consumers demand options. But this poses a problem. Scripture and tradition tell us that formation into the likeness of Christ is not accomplished by always getting what we want. In ages past, choice was not heralded as a Christian's right. In fact, relinquishing our choices by submitting to a spiritual mentor or community was seen as a prerequisite for growth in Christ. Shepherds guided believers through formative and corrective disciplines, most of them activities we would never choose to engage in if left to our desires. But surrendering control ensured we received what we needed to mature in Christ, not simply what we wanted.

In consumer-Christianity, however, church leaders function as divine baristas, supplying spiritual goods and services for people to choose from based on their personal desires. And our concern becomes not whether people are growing, but whether they are satisfied—often measured by attendance and giving. An unhappy member, like an unhappy customer, will find satisfaction someplace else. As one Church, Inc. pastor enthusiastically said, "The problem with blended services is that half the people are happy half the time. With a video venue, you can say, 'If you don't like this service style, try another one!'"

Ironically, the demand for choice that has fueled Church, Inc. may ultimately be its undoing. According to George Barna's book *Revolution*, twenty million Americans are no longer satisfied with the options available to them at institutional churches. Instead they are "choosing from a proliferation of options, weaving together a set of favored alternatives into a unique tapestry that constitutes the personal 'church' of the individual."[10]

Rather than engaging one congregation, the new breed of Christian consumers customize their discipleship the way we customize a playlist. They might find encouragement at a community support group, worship at a Christian concert, listen to a podcast sermon, and be equipped for evangelism via a campus ministry. Meanwhile the church as we've known it fades into memory like vinyl LPs and compact discs.

Ultimately, our greatest concern should not be consumerism's erosion of the church, but its commodification of God Himself. Prior to the Industrial Revolution, most of the food, clothing, tools, and furniture people used were made at home or by someone nearby. Every item had a story and person attached to it known by its user. A rocking chair had value not only for its comfort, but because Uncle John made it.

Today, as I sit in my favorite armchair at Starbucks enjoying my tea, I have no idea who assembled the chair, who grew the tea leaves, or who designed the cup—I barely know the guy with the nose ring behind the counter who poured the hot water. Consumerism has stripped the goods we use every day from their context; they have no story or value apart from my consumption of them.

Tragically, a consumer worldview has led us to commodify parts of God's creation far more valuable than chairs and teabags. Sexuality, for example, is commodified through pornography and human trafficking. People are reduced to objects of self-gratification to be discarded when no longer desired. Human life is commodified through abortion. An unborn child no longer has any value apart from what a mother chooses to give him or her.

In our society, the only value an object has is the value I give it. A commodity exists to satisfy my desire and supply my needs—nothing more. Because consumerism has formed us to engage both goods and people this way, it should surprise no one that in our culture God also has no value apart from what He can do for me.

Christian Smith, a leading sociologist of religion, has received a lot of attention for his research on the spiritual lives of American teens. He concluded that the faith of most teenagers, including the majority of those who attend evangelical churches, is MTD: Moralistic Therapeutic Deism. Smith explains:

> By "moralistic" I mean oriented toward being good and nice. . . .
>
> By "therapeutic" I mean being primarily concerned with one's own happiness . . . in contrast to, say, a focus on glorifying God, learning obedience, or serving others.
>
> Finally, by "deism" I mean a view of God as normally distant and not involved in one's life, except . . . if one has a problem one needs God to solve. . . . in other words, God functions as a combination divine butler and cosmic therapist.[11]

Smith found that most teenagers hold this self-centered perception of God because it is the faith most American adults have as well.

This deity of consumerism shows no resemblance to the Consuming Fire described in Scripture. People may say they believe in Jesus, but the archaic Lord who calls forth sacrifice, promises suffering in this life, and demands obedience for His glory—and whom Karl Barth described as "wholly other"—He is not what they have in mind. They're thinking of the Jesus that adorns T-shirts and SUV tailgates.

Any resentment I had toward Greg and Margaret after our conversation at Starbucks waned quickly. Like many others at my church, they were simply doing what they had been formed to do. I may as well be angry at a fish for swimming. Immersed in a consumer culture, Greg and Margaret were living like consumers—making decisions, including spiritual ones, based on personal desires and convenience.

The truth is I failed Greg and Margaret. During the years they were at my church, I failed to teach them that the core values of consumerism were incongruent with the Christian life. The satisfaction of our desires is not the goal of life. The church does not exist to supply spiritual goods and services to religious consumers. And God is not a commodity that exists to make you feel better.

Perhaps I failed Greg and Margaret because my identity has been formed by consumerism, too. Maybe I was too busy being a marketer, sales rep, and spiritual barista to be a pastor dedicated to protecting Greg and Margaret from the 3,500 wolves in sheep's clothing they encounter every day. Whatever the reason, because of my failure, that responsibility now rests with shepherds in another pasture.

REFLECTION AND APPLICATION

How have you allowed the values of our consumer culture to shape your approach to ministry? Which of these consumer values do you see as innocuous, and which are harmful to the formation of faithful disciples? How can you tell the difference?

We cannot escape from the pervasive reality of the consumer culture, but what is something you can do to help those you lead recognize and respond faithfully to its deforming power?

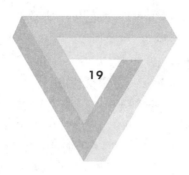

WITNESS

19

A FEW YEARS AGO I saw a movie—my wife chose it—called *Shall We Dance?* One of the characters had an insightful monologue about the meaning of marriage. She said:

> We need a witness to our lives. There's a billion people on the planet. I mean, what does any one life really mean? But in a marriage you're promising to care about everything. The good things, the bad things, the terrible things, the mundane things . . . all of it, all of the time, every day. You're saying, "Your life will not go unnoticed, because I will notice it. Your life will not go unwitnessed, because I will be your witness."

Her intent in the film was to explain the companionship we long for in marriage, but I think the fear of living an unnoticed life also explains the powerful appeal of social media.

At a recent conference for college students, a pastor told sixty thousand young people, "The only thing I'm afraid of is living an insignificant life." That fear resonates with many of us, but in our exhibitionist culture we've been formed to believe that significance comes from being noticed. This explains both our culture's deification of celebrities and disregard for the unborn. Celebrities are valued merely because they are seen by millions, while unborn babies are unvalued because they haven't yet been seen by anyone. Our culture has embraced the cliché that out of sight really is out of mind.

But as church leaders, we are tempted, perhaps more than others, to believe that our value is defined by the visible, quantifiable, and tweetable aspects of our lives.

Most of us strive toward the eternal life of celebrity but live closer to the second death of obscurity, and in this struggle we've come to see social media as a savior. With each new Facebook friend or Twitter follower, we gain another witness to our lives, another person to notice us and thereby add another particle of validation to our existence. Each "retweet" or "like" brings an ephemeral happiness because someone is saying, "You matter. Your life is being noticed."

If this is at least part of the lure of social media, what are we to conclude about the disproportionate presence of pastors on Twitter? The site has proven to be so popular among church leaders that Twitter hired a senior executive with the task of targeting and recruiting more pastors. Yes, it can be another way of communicating with our congregations Monday through Saturday, but might we be looking for something more? Might we be looking for more witnesses? More significance?

We may be seeking to fulfill a spiritual hunger for companionship that cannot be satisfied online. In fact, at its deepest level, it cannot even be met through the intimacy of marriage. Our yearning for significance and our desperation for a witness can only be quenched by God. Psalm 139 tells us that God knows us in a manner no other can. He sees every facet of our lives, and He witnesses every thought and moment even before they occur.

In the economy of God's kingdom, there is not a single thought, feeling, or moment that is lost. Nothing is unseen or unrecorded. God is our witness. But as church leaders, we are tempted, perhaps more than others, to believe that our value is defined by the visible, quantifiable, and tweetable aspects of our lives. How many came? How many followed? How many liked? This is a soul-crushing mistake, and is perhaps why we struggle with prayer. Prayer, which is our private communion with God, is not something others can see. In prayer only God is our witness, and in prayer only God is our reward.

Rather than tweeting incessantly, what if we followed Paul's advice and learned to pray incessantly? Thomas Kelly wrote about this kind of life. He said:

There is a way of ordering our mental life on more than one level at once. On one level we may be thinking, discussing, seeing, calculating, meeting all the demands of external affairs. But deep within, behind the scenes, at a profounder level, we may also be in prayer and adoration, song and worship and a gentle receptiveness to divine breathings.[1]

The world today only values and pursues the first level. It believes what others can see and retweet is what really matters. It says the most important thing is being noticed. But, as Kelly notes, "We know that the deep level of prayer is the most important thing in the world. It is at this deep level that the real business of life is determined."

REFLECTION AND APPLICATION

In the ancient world, the faithful fasted regularly from food to loosen their dependence on physical nourishment and deepen their intimacy with God. Consider what a social media fast might do for your communion with God, and how regularly silencing the voices online might help you hear the voice of your heavenly Father more.

Why are you on social media? What are you really looking for? How are you taking legitimate needs intended to be satisfied through friendship, marriage, or communion with God and seeking a faster but ultimately less nourishing fix on social media?

20

TECHNOLOGY

OUR FAMILY WAS standing among thousands of others in front of Cinderella's castle at Walt Disney World. Music soared, lifting our spirits, and nearly our feet, off the ground. Fireworks turned the night into day, and the entire facade of the castle came alive with projected images. My eyes couldn't track fast enough. The air was heavy with sweat and sweets.

If a more immersive, stimulating spectacle is possible, I haven't found it. But not everyone was enthralled. Next to me in the crowd was a boy, about ten years old, pecking on a screen inches from his eyes, oblivious to the hurricane of light, sound, and color around him. His body was at Disney World, but his mind was lost in the immaterial world of pixels. As I looked over the crowd, I saw many other kids—and some parents—focused on screens rather than the present spectacle. If this isn't enough to get their attention, I thought, nothing ever will. That was when I realized we had entered the age of dis-incarnation.

When Jesus came to dwell among us, the apostle Paul says, He "emptied himself" to take on flesh. This means He willingly set aside some of His divine attributes, like omnipresence, to occupy a physical body. Scripture tells us that God is spirit and is therefore unconfined. "O Lord . . . where shall I flee from your presence?" asked David (Ps. 139:1, 7). When Jesus became an incarnate man, however, He was not everywhere, doing everything, or engaging everyone. He accepted the confinement of a body. To be incarnate is necessarily limiting.

Technology, however, offers us the illusion of omnipresence. It allows us to escape the physical limitations of our bodies to transport ourselves elsewhere. In an instant I can flee the boredom of standing in line at the DMV to text my brother in California, or lose myself in highlights from last night's Bulls game. I no longer have to be present with those near me, or even with my own thoughts, thanks to the genie in my pocket. Our phones have become totems that grant us the godlike power to escape our bodies, but in the process are we losing some of our humanity?

This temptation may be especially strong for ministers of the Word. We have a divinely ordained mission; why shouldn't we employ godlike technology to accomplish it? Technology promises to help us reach more people more easily than we could ever do as embodied ministers. The analog, incarnate ministry of the past was slow. The word was transmitted person-to-person, face-to-face. The care of souls required shepherds to be physically present with their sheep. How agrarian.

With the advent of digital, dis-incarnate ministry, our mission can finally industrialize. Now we, not just the tele-vangelists, can all scale our influence and preach to thousands via pixels on a screen. We can manufacture disciples via blogs and tweets and live-stream ourselves to our anonymous sheep anytime, anywhere. Dis-incarnate ministry is so much cleaner, so much more efficient, and infinitely more marketable. In Jesus, the Word became flesh, and for ages the church followed that pattern, but our generation has finally set the Word free from the inherent limits of incarnation. Our Lord must be grateful to us.

The only ones inhibiting this more efficient form of ministry are those who stubbornly refuse to abandon their bodies. For example, a few years ago I preached a message about forgiving our enemies. I could see a young woman near the front struggling throughout the sermon; her husband comforted her with his arm around her shoulder. (Had I preached via video, I wouldn't have seen her at all.)

After the message I went to speak with her. (Another expectation of incarnate ministry.) I learned that a man had broken into her apartment and sexually assaulted her. He had been caught and convicted for the crime, but she was deeply wounded emotionally and physically. "I

> Jesus became incarnate to redeem every part of us—mind, soul, and body. Ministry in His name must do the same.

don't know if I can forgive him," she said. I took her and her husband's hands, and together we prayed.

Standing with this broken young woman, I realized that evil makes no distinction between our bodies and us. How, then, in our call to overcome evil, can we make that distinction? Jesus became incarnate to redeem every part of us—mind, soul, and body. Ministry in His name must do the same. Learning the way of Jesus means accepting, and even embracing, our embodied limitations. It means emptying ourselves of the desire to be everywhere, do everything, and engage everyone, and instead be fully present for the spectacle of redemption happening right where we are.

REFLECTION AND APPLICATION

After a discussion with leaders in your community or organization, develop a plan for the use of technology. Where will it be employed? Where will it be excluded? How will you create oases from screens where people can be present with the Lord and one another? What questions will you ask to determine the use or absence of technology for a given setting?

How has your ministry already become dis-incarnate? What benefits do you gain by not being present with the people you lead? What is Jesus asking you to set aside in order to dwell with His people?

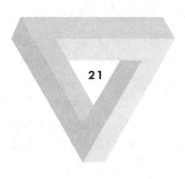

JUSTICE

INDUSTRIALIZATION works because of specialization. Consider Henry Ford's innovation of the assembly line. Rather than hiring craftsmen to build automobiles, which required hard-to-find workers with multiple skills, Ford found a way to manufacture complicated machines with cheap, unskilled workers by having each person specialize in a single repeatable skill. By breaking goods down to their component parts, more goods would be made and more efficiently.

This drive toward specialization is also evident within Church, Inc. Rather than embracing the fullness of God's kingdom and His mission in the world, our instinct is to atomize it into its components. Then we often argue with one another about which of these parts is most foundational. Nowhere is this more evident today than in the ongoing debate between advocates of evangelism and social justice.

The question is difficult to avoid as voices from all sides fill conference stages, blogs, and even the pages of ministry journals. One side believes social action was unjustifiably divorced from gospel mission a century ago during the Modernist-Fundamentalist Controversy. What God has joined together, they argue, we have wrongly put asunder.

Voices on the other side recognize the goodness of seeking peace and wholeness for the suffering, but not at the expense of eternal salvation. They believe social justice to be an implication of the gospel, but not central to it. Failure to make such a distinction, they fear, will lead the church down the slippery slope of theological liberalism. Justice may be an accessory on the assembly line of disciples within Church, Inc., but it's not the chassis of evangelism.

As I encounter this debate in various ministry forums, what surprises me is the lack of historical or global thought admitted into the discussion. We seem to think this is a purely contemporary, and primarily American, question. And one can sometimes detect a hint of smugness among my own generation of younger leaders as we congratulate ourselves for rescuing social justice from an evangelical phantom zone, where we assume it had been languishing until we came along.

Nothing could be further from the truth.

The church has been addressing matters of mission and justice since Pentecost. The book of Acts, after all, isn't just a list of evangelistic sermons. The issue is also repeatedly found among the patristic writings. My own understanding of how evangelism and social justice intersect has been greatly informed by a more recent church father, John Stott. Stott, whose service to the Lord in this age ended in 2011, was neither American nor a Gen-Xer. He was English, Anglican, and a theological heavyweight of twentieth century evangelicalism. Together with Billy Graham he established the Lausanne Movement, and he chaired the drafting committee for the Lausanne Covenant, one of the most respected and widely accepted modern statements of Christian faith and mission.

Having witnessed the many horrors of the twentieth century, John Stott also wrestled greatly with the question of evangelism and social action. What he concluded has much to say to us in the twenty-first century. In short, Stott believed both sides of the controversy were in error.

In his book *Christian Mission in the Modern World*, Stott argues that most people try to make social justice either superior or subordinate to evangelism. The superior position diminishes the importance of calling people to be reconciled to God through Christ—something Stott found utterly incongruent with the New Testament. The subordinate position, however, he found equally untenable. It made social action into a PR device, a way to win favor leading to conversion, a mere means to an end. Stott wrote, "In its most blatant form this makes social work . . . the sugar on the pill, the bait on the hook, while in its best form it gives to the gospel a credibility it would otherwise lack. In either case the smell of hypocrisy hangs round our philanthropy."[1]

Stott came to recognize that forcing every facet of the

Christian life into a mission or evangelism framework simply wouldn't stand, and asking whether evangelism or justice matters more misses the point entirely. Instead he concluded that social justice and evangelism "belong to each other and yet are independent of each other. Each stands on its own feet in its own right alongside the other. Neither is a means to the other, or even a manifestation of the other. For each is an end in itself."

Therefore, according to Stott, our participation in social action is not fueled by a missional imperative, evangelistic pragmatism, or even theological certitude, "but rather simple, uncomplicated compassion. Love has no need to justify itself."[2]

Is John Stott's writing enough to settle the debate over evangelism and social justice in every congregation? Maybe not. But what he does offer is another path into, and out of, the controversy. As you engage with other leaders around this question, and as you talk with your own community about it, don't get snared by the false dichotomy declaring that either evangelism or social justice must be superior. Let's affirm every work God has called His servants to, whether that's proclaiming reconciliation or demonstrating it, as long as His love is found fueling it.

Which side of the artificial evangelism/social justice divide are you more likely to fall on? How do you unintentionally place certain elements of God's work above others or diminish other Christians' callings?

Whichever element is weaker in your community—justice or evangelism—develop a plan with other leaders to intentionally strengthen it. How can you affirm the dignity of those motivated by Christ's love toward their neighbors' needs?

MISSIONALISM

"THERE IS A FIRST-RATE commitment to a second-rate mission." That is what Roger, a leader in global church planting, said as he looked at the rock climbers ascending a cliff in the Alps. Many of us called into ministry feel the same way. Rather than giving our lives to climbing a rock, building a business, or amassing a fortune, we are committed to what really matters: a first-rate mission—advancing the gospel and the church of Jesus Christ.

But what if we're wrong?

Roger spent decades serving Christ, planting churches on four continents. But after reflecting on his labor for the kingdom of God, his confession surprised many of us. "I've given most of my energy to a second-rate mission as well," he said. "Don't get me wrong. Church planting is great. But someday that mission will end. My first calling is to live with God. That must be my first commitment."

What Roger articulated was a temptation that many in ministry face. To put it simply, many church leaders unknowingly replace the transcendent vitality of a life *with* God for the ego satisfaction they derive from a life *for* God. Before exploring how this shift occurs in church leaders, let me take a step or two backwards and explain how I have seen it in the Christian college students I've worked with in recent years.

As graduation draws near, many students begin to worry about life after school. In my conversations they often speak about a desire to "make a difference in the world" and the great fear of living an "insignificant" life. It's remarkable how much has changed since the days where a good-paying job with benefits was considered a victory after college. Now anything short of changing the world is a failure. I've come to recognize, however, that when a student says, "What should I do with my life?" there is actually a deeper, unspoken question on her mind: "How can I prove I am valuable?"

In the chapter about ambition, we've already seen how a deep fear of insignificance can fuel great achievement. It may be presented to the world as godly ambition and a passionate desire for God's mission, but in truth we are desperately trying to win the praise and approval of both God and people. This intermingling of God's mission with prideful ambition (when well hidden) can win a person great acclaim within Christian communities, and it can produce genuine good in the world as people are aided by the works we accomplish. However, when we are motivated by fear more than love, and driven by our ego more than Christ's Spirit, a never ending drive to prove our value can consume us.

Gordon MacDonald calls this darker side to ministry "missionalism." It is "the belief that the *worth* of one's life is determined by the achievement of a grand objective." He continues:

> Missionalism starts slowly and gains a foothold in the leader's attitude. Before long the mission controls almost everything: time, relationships, health, spiritual depth, ethics, and convictions. . . . In advanced stages, missionalism means doing whatever it takes to solve the problem. In its worst iteration, the end always justifies the means. The family goes; health is sacrificed; integrity is jeopardized; God-connection is limited.[1]

I have seen the early symptoms of missionalism in many college students. They first encountered the malady as kids within the evangelical subculture that explicitly and implicitly communicated that a person's value was linked to their missional achievements. When this message eventually combines with the insecurities of young adulthood, it can lead a student to make decision about their future that are incongruent with their gifts or callings all in the pursuit of significance.

Sometimes I encounter the affects of missionalism after it has metastasized throughout a church leader's life. To identify its presence I will sometimes ask, "What motivates you to stay away from the temptations of sin?" The answer I often hear, the answer most pastors have been conditioned to say, is, "I wouldn't want to do anything to jeopardize my ministry." That response often reveals where a leader's true devotion is. Sadly, I rarely hear a pastor say, "I wouldn't want anything to disrupt my communion with God." So few of us have been given a vision of a life *with* Christ, and instead we seek to fill the void with a vision for ministry—a vision of a life *for* Christ.

Phil Vischer, the creator of VeggieTales, had his faith formed in a missionalism environment. He said the heroes of his evangelical community were "the Rockefellers of the Christian world," ministers who were enterprising, effective, and who made a huge impact for God. His own grandfather and great-grandfather were among them. This led Vischer to conclude that what God desired from him was world-changing impact. "God would never call us from greater impact to lesser impact!" he wrote. "How many kids did you invite to Sunday school? How many souls have you won? How big is your church? How many people will be in heaven because of your efforts? Impact, man!"

But after losing his company in 2003, Vischer began to rethink the message of missionalism he had ingested as a younger man.

> The more I dove into Scripture, the more I realized I had been deluded. I had grown up drinking a dangerous cocktail—a mix of the gospel, the Protestant work ethic, and the American dream.

My eternal value was rooted in what I could accomplish. . . . The Savior I was following seemed,
in hindsight, equal parts Jesus, Ben Franklin, and
Henry Ford.[2]

Vischer's experience matches what I've heard some pastors say after a few decades of carrying missionalism's heavy
yoke. One pastor in his thirties put it this way:

The church is growing, and there's excitement
everywhere. But personally I feel less and less good
about what I'm doing. I'm restless and tired. I ask
myself how long I can keep this all up. Why is
my touch with God so limited? Why am I feeling
guilty about where my marriage is? When did this
stop being fun?

What may be most sinister about missionalism is its
self-propagating mechanism. When a church leader is in
its grip, he or she will unknowingly transmit the burden
of missionalism to those under their care. When a pastor's
sense of significance is linked to the impact of their ministry, those within the church are told the same message. In
subtle or overt ways they are rewarded for their missional
output or shamed for their failure to perform, and a new
generation of Christian missionalists are created. After a
few generations the values of missionalism may be so in-
grained within the culture of a church or denomination
that they are never questioned. A careful examination of
the community may reveal that pastors are imploding at

alarming rates, young people are full of anxiety, families may be in crisis, and the fruit of God's Spirit may be woefully absent, but no one stops. No one dares ask if something is wrong, or if this is what God had intended for His people. No one questions the enshrinement of missionalism because the work must go on. Impact, man!

You may be thinking, "But we are called to do things for God. And what's the alternative—continuing to allow the people in our churches to be self-consumed Christians seeking only their comfort?" That is a very fair concern. And I completely concur that the consumer posture is choking much of the modern church, both in North America and increasingly around the globe.

But the prescribed solution I hear in many ministry settings is to transform people from consumer Christians into activist Christians. The exact direction of the activism may depend on one's theological and ecclesiological orientation. For traditional evangelicals, it's all about evangelism—getting believers to share their faith, give to overseas missions, and grow the church. For many younger Christians, the focus might be compassion and justice—digging wells and eradicating poverty. But what both groups agree on is that we are to devote our lives to, and derive our significance from, God's mission, however we may define it.

Please don't think I am trying to dismiss the importance of the *missio dei* or the church's part within it. Like other church leaders, I greatly desire to see more Christians hear God's call and engage in the good, life-saving work He has given us. And I am incredibly grateful for my friends in ministry who have awakened the church to the theological and practical necessity of mission in our age. But as Tim Keller has deftly observed, "An idol is a good thing made into an ultimate thing."

The temptation within activist streams of Christianity is to put the good mission of God into the place God alone should occupy. The irony is that in our desire to draw people away from the selfishness of consumer Christianity, we may simply be replacing one idol with another.

In my work, I attend or participate in a lot of ministry conferences. You know how those typically go. A thousand pastors gather at a resort for two days to have a "life-changing experience." They herd into the hotel's main ballroom, bags of complimentary books and Chick-fil-A gift cards in hand, where their internal organs are realigned by the worship band's bass-thumping versions of classic Christian hymns. After which the celebrity pastor speaker will fire up the crowd with a call to "change the world for Christ," "impact a generation with the gospel," or "spark a revival in the church."

We've all gotten used to hearing how we're going to change the church/culture/generation/world. I call it the MOAB Doctrine: "Change the world through massive cultural upheaval and high-impact tactics." MOAB (Mother Of All Bombs) is the nickname of the largest non-nuclear bomb in the US military's arsenal. When impact is more important than precision, there's nothing better.

Likewise, the MOAB Doctrine is an approach to ministry that values massive impact and visibility above all else.

This shock-and-awe approach to ministry is extremely attractive to those shaped by missionalism. The temptation is never explicit but always present: by making a huge impact you can convince the world of God's legitimacy as well as your own.

Sadly, the church has so accepted this idea that it is often the very reason we are drawn to ministry. We create an atmosphere in which young people may be attracted to ministry roles—not out of a genuine calling that emerges from their communion with Christ, but out of a desire to be significant and valued by a community that honors missional effectiveness above all else. We draw them to pastoral ministry from a shadow desire for significance, honor, prestige, or ambition rooted in self rather than Christ. And once they enter ministry, the pattern continues. Now that they've chosen the "right" vocation, they have to prove it by having a big impact.

But what concerns me is that a MOAB view of ministry leaves no space for failure. It cannot tolerate a theology of ineffectiveness. So what is a pastor without impact supposed to do? How do we reconcile our desire for impact with our failure to produce it? If my legitimacy is linked to my impact, does a lack of impact mean I am an illegitimate pastor, an unfit minister?

These questions tap into the core of our identity, and when it comes under attack, we will do nearly anything to protect ourselves or nurse our pain. Why are we seeing an epidemic of pornography and other addictive behaviors among church leaders? Why do ministry families struggle so deeply and secretly? Why do so many of us struggle with anger, jealousy, and resentment in our church roles? There are many causes, but these outcomes are not accidental. We have created a system that attracts us to ministry for the wrong reason, motivates us with the idol of mission, and then leaves us bloody and wounded when we fail to meet our own expectations. As Dallas Willard was fond of saying, "Your system is perfectly designed to produce the results you are getting." Our church culture is designed to attract, consume, and eject pastors. It is built for failure. Ironically, it refuses to give us a redemptive theology of failure in the process.

This is the great danger of endlessly extolling the importance of the mission—it put can place God's mission ahead of God Himself. A healthy leader will not confuse their calling and their values. Paul, for example, did not make this mistake. He understood that his calling—to be a messenger to the Gentiles—was not the same as his treasure: to be united with Christ. His communion with Christ rooted and preceded his work for Him.

Few passages of Scripture illustrate our present dilemma better than the parable of the prodigal son in Luke 15. The young son did not desire a relationship with his father, he simply wanted his father's wealth—a poignant example of the consumer Christian. He took the money, left home, and indulged in self-centered and consumeristic living. Eventually he was broke and desperate. When the son returned home everyone was shocked to see his father joyfully running to embrace the rebellious son with open arms.

The lesson for us, however, is more rooted in the example of the older son. He did not find his value in the pursuit of self-indulgent desires, but in faithfully serving his father. When he learned that his father had welcomed his younger brother home with open arms, however, he was furious. The son refused to enter the house or join the celebration.

The father begged the older son to come to the party. But the son refused. "Look, these many years I have served you, and I never disobeyed your command, yet you never gave me a young goat, that I might celebrate with my friends. But when this son of yours came, who has devoured your property with prostitutes, you killed the fattened calf for him!" (Luke 15:29–30).

With these words the older son reveals where he rooted his significance: "All these years I have served you, and I never disobeyed your command." The older son was devoted to his work, to his achievement, to his father's business and mission. And for his faithful effort the older son was expecting a reward; a public acknowledgment of his hard work and the esteem of the whole community for his service. In this regard he was the same as the younger son. Neither boy was primarily focused upon a relationship with the father; instead both were focused on what they might get from him.

It's important to remember that Jesus told this parable to a gathering of Pharisees and scribes—devoted religious leaders who drew their significance from their obedience to God. Jesus is not condemning commitment to God's mission, but he was warning about the dangers of finding our significance and value in it rather than in God Himself. Jesus is not diminishing the older son's service, just as He is not endorsing the younger son's sinfulness. Rather, He is showing that both religious consumerism and religious activism fail to capture what God truly desires for His people. Pouring ourselves into God's mission is not our highest calling. For that we must look more closely at the father's response to the older son in the parable.

"Son, you are always with me, and all that is mine is yours. It was fitting to celebrate and be glad, for this your brother was dead, and is alive; he was lost, and is found" (Luke 15:31–32).

It's remarkable that the father never mentions the older son's years of service, just as he never speaks of the younger son's rebelliousness when he returned home. Instead, the father's focus is all about having his son with him. While the sons were fixated on the father's wealth, the father was fixated on his children. This is what they both failed to understand, and it is what both Christian consumerism and Christian missionalism fail to see. God's gifts are a blessing and His work is vital, but neither can nor should replace God Himself as our first calling.

While a vision for serving God is needed, and the desperate condition of our world cannot be ignored, there is a higher calling going unanswered in many Christian communities. As shepherds of God's people, we must not allow our fears of insignificance to drive us into an unrelenting pursuit of church growth, cultural impact, or missional activism. Instead, we must model for our people a first-class commitment to a first-class purpose—living in perpetual communion with God Himself. As we embrace the call to live with God, only then will we be capable of illuminating such a life for our people.

REFLECTION AND APPLICATION

How are you tempted to exchange a life-giving communion with God for a world-changing mission for God? Does a vision of God or His work fill your imagination as you daydream or pray?

Vischer spoke about having his vision of faith shaped by "a mix of the gospel, the Protestant work ethic, and the American dream." Who or what has formed your understanding of faith and mission? Are you able to acknowledge what parts may be incongruent with the call of Christ?

23

HEALTH

MY FATHER IS a doctor. When I was growing up, he hoped that I would follow in his steps, so he often shared stories about the wonders of his profession. Like the day when he cracked a case that had stumped other doctors for weeks. It turned out to be a parasite acquired in the South Pacific during World War II. "The man had a dormant worm in his gut for over fifty years!" my dad exclaimed with a victorious smile on his face. "Medicine is amazing." A few nights later, however, he would point his index finger at me and declare in exhaustion, "Never become a doctor. You just stick your finger up people's rear ends all day."

Message received. I became a pastor.

When I was eighteen, my father learned what it was like to be on the receiving end of a latex glove. He was diagnosed with cancer. His type was very survivable if caught early—which could only be known through surgery.

I sat next to him in the waiting room before the operation. It was odd seeing him in a hospital not striding with confidence into a patient's room or giving orders at a nurses' station like a battleship commander—something I had witnessed many times as a boy accompanying him on Saturday morning rounds. Instead he sat in silence with his shoulders rolled and hands shaking.

"You know doctors make the worst patients," he said.

"Why?" I asked.

"Because we know too much," he answered. "We know the thousands of things that can go wrong that most people never imagine."

Thankfully the cancer was caught early and he survived, but something important happened when the physician became the patient. He gained something that can't be taught in medical school or acquired from years of practicing medicine. Cancer gave him empathy. I saw his compassion and understanding for his patients grow following his own health crisis. Doctors may make the worst patients, but patients make the best doctors.

Like medicine, ministry is a calling that requires both knowledge and skills. Many of us have spent years, even decades, studying Scripture, theology, history, and culture to faithfully connect God's Word to our world. We've also learned to counsel and shepherd our congregations toward life with Christ. Within our churches this makes us the experts, the go-to people, when others have a struggle or need advice.

Sure, we have our moments of self-pity when we complain about the tedious tasks of ministry—the ecclesiastical rectal exams we must administer day after day. If we're honest, however, having people seek our help is an arrangement that can serve their needs and feed our sense of importance simultaneously. Over time, our status—in our churches and in our heads—can grow to an unhealthy level. It may also cause us to believe the key to successful ministry is always having the right answers and advancing our knowledge and skills so that everyone who seeks our help can receive it. This need to maintain our position as the expert can, ironically, prevent us from acquiring the quality that the very best Christian leaders possess—empathy. We are happy to play the role of savior, but we don't want to be identified as sinners.

> When we face our fears and experience the healing pain of sanctification, we gain empathy for the sinners we are called to shepherd.

We may sense there's something amiss in our souls or suspect that our descent into sin is becoming chronic, but the thought of opening ourselves to examination is too terrifying. We know the risks better than most. We've seen the carnage of broken lives in our offices and in tear-filled family rooms. We'd rather avoid the humiliation and let the cancer silently grow.

Still, there is a gift awaiting leaders who humble themselves. When we face our fears and experience the healing pain of sanctification, we gain empathy for the sinners we are called to shepherd. We will exhibit greater compassion for the next unhealthy person who wants to talk to the pastor on Monday morning, or the disruptive woman in the worship service, or the addicted man who fails at recovery yet again.

I've found that my empathy grows most when I step away from the "expert" spotlight. That means regularly not preaching and using someone else's teaching to examine my soul. It also means having regular checkups with godly men who care deeply for me and my health. I have also found the Ignatian prayers of Examen to be an indispensable tool of self-awareness. They make Psalm 139:23 a practiced reality: "Search me, O God, and know my heart! Try me and know my thoughts!"

Pastors make the worst sinners, but sinners make the best pastors.

REFLECTION AND APPLICATION

Where can you abandon the identity of "the expert"? Are there settings or relationships that allow you to be vulnerable? If so, how can you increase your engagement with them? If not, what fear is keeping you isolated and unknown?

Invite everyone in your leadership team to identify the settings and relationships of transparency in their lives. Where are they not "the pastor"?

24

REHABILITATION

the hospital room, I pulled the patient's chart from the nurses' station, so I knew I was about to enter the room of a fifty-four-year-old male with multiple arm, shoulder, and facial fractures. I had been conditioned by my chaplain supervisor to silently repeat a phrase whenever I held the handle of a hospital room door: "When I enter this room, I represent the presence of God." It was an intimidating and ill-fitting role for a twenty-six-year-old, like wearing someone else's suit—someone with more gray hair and gravitas.

I entered and introduced myself as the chaplain. Bill was immobilized, his arm and shoulder in a cast and his face badly bruised and swollen. He gently turned his head to look at me.

"I can't talk very well," he said through clenched teeth. "They've wired my jaw shut."

"I understand you took a nasty fall yesterday. What happened?"

"I don't remember," Bill said. "I was drunk." His speech was difficult to understand, so I drew my chair closer to his head.

"You're young," he said. He suspected I was wearing someone else's suit, too.

"I'm a seminary student," I said. Bill looked away, his eyes wet. I assumed his pain meds were wearing off.

"You're here to talk about God?"

"If you'd like to," I said, "or we can talk about whatever's on your mind."

"I used to talk to people about God," Bill said. "I'm a pastor." I tried to hide my surprise.

He was now crying steadily. I moved the tissue box closer to his mobile arm.

"When I was your age I never thought I would end up here—like this. I've lost everything. Everything. My ministry, my marriage, my kids."

Through tears and clenched teeth, Bill confessed his sins and his alcoholism. Despite my training and experience with hundreds of patients, including any number of alcoholics, I was lost for words.

"Take a good look at me," Bill said. "Don't make the same mistakes. Don't end up like me." With almost no prompting, he began to share at length about his life and his struggles, laced with warnings and advice for the green seminarian at his bedside. Maybe he opened up to me because I had never known Pastor Bill, the strong Christian leader. I only saw Alcoholic Bill, the broken hospital patient. Unlike his congregation or family, I could only assume what his life used to be, and maybe in his mind that made me safer and my unspoken judgments slightly more tolerable.

"Are you married?" he asked.

"Yes," I said.

"Kids?"

"Not yet."

"There's nothing more important than your family," he said. "The church is not more important." He talked about his experience as a pastor, the stresses he faced, the pressures of running a church, and the solace he sought in alcohol. As I listened to Bill's advice, I felt that he wasn't really talking to me but to a younger version of himself. He looked at me and saw his past. I looked at him and wondered—am I looking at my future?

How many times had he stood authoritatively before a congregation to lead them in worship? Now he lay helpless in a hospital bed of his own making. How many people had looked up to him with respect and admiration? Now he was looked down upon with pity or contempt. How many divine truths had he boldly preached from the pulpit? Now his mouth was wired shut with only confessions leaking out in muddled whispers. Lying in his bed, Bill reminded me of the classic cartoon version of *The Lion, the Witch, and the Wardrobe* I had watched repeatedly as a boy, where Aslan is on the stone table bound, shaved, and muzzled. The mighty lion taunted by his enemies as a mere pussycat.

Over our hour together, I saw that Bill's bones were

broken by more than a fall, and his life was fractured by more than alcoholism. There were deeper forces tearing on him, and they weren't finished yet. His story was filled with self-loathing and shame. He was deeply embarrassed. He saw the sum of his life as nothing more than a warning sign, a tragic morality tale to keep other ministers on the straight path. All of it pointed to an invisible wound no orthopedic surgeon could mend. Bill had lost his dignity.

One of my favorite films is *Birdman of Alcatraz* (1962). It's the fictionalized retelling of the story of Robert Stroud, a defiant prisoner who studied and nursed injured birds in his cell. After decades in prison, Stroud never conformed to the rigid expectations of the warden. The tension between the two reached a climax near the end of the film with this exchange:

> Warden: Not once have you ever shown a sign of rehabilitation.

> Stroud: Rehabilitation. I wonder if you know what the word means. Do you?

> Warden: Don't be insulting.

> Stroud: *The Unabridged Webster's International Dictionary* says it comes from the Latin root *habilis*. The definition is "to invest again with dignity." Do you consider that part of your job, Harvey,

to give a man back the dignity he once had? Your
only interest is in how he behaves. You told me
that once a long time ago and I'll never forget it.
"You'll conform to our ideas of how you should
behave." And you haven't retreated from that stand
one inch in 35 years. You want your prisoners to
dance out the gates like puppets on a string with
rubber stamp values impressed by you. With your
sense of conformity. Your sense of behavior. Even
your sense of morality. That's why you're a failure,
Harvey. . . . Because you rob prisoners of the most
important thing in their lives—their individuality.[1]

This sinful world inflicts a lot of damage, but its most
insidious evil is to rob us of our dignity. Every other attack is won outside a person. It can throw hatred, injustice,
poverty, or physical pain at us, and the strong may endure
these trials without losing their sense of worth. But if the
world can convince a person he is worthless, that he is un-
deserving of love, then no amount of external well-being
will repair what has been stolen from him.

That's what I sensed in Bill. He saw himself as worthless,
a failure, and utterly deserving of his pathetic circumstances.
He certainly was not the first, or the last, patient I met who
had a shattered sense of dignity, but what made him particularly tragic were his decades within the church—the very
place where broken souls ought to find rehabilitation. And
even worse, Bill was a leader within the church. How could
a man with access to so much theology, so much Scripture

and sacrament, and so many helpful resources not have found restoration?

Unfortunately, like Robert Stroud in the federal prison system, many people do not experience the church as a community of rehabilitation. Far from restoring a person's dignity, the church may actually take it from them, as Bill painfully testified from his hospital bed. Like a prison, Church, Inc. is about systems, efficiencies, and metrics. It sees ministry as an industry and churches as factories that produce disciples on an assembly line of sermons and music and programs. The goal is to have disciples "dance out" the church door "like puppets on a string with rubber stamp values." This dehumanizing, impersonal structure expects conformity and therefore robs both ministers and the ministered of their individuality.

Rather than rehabilitating what the world has stolen from us, Church, Inc. only compounds our shame by adding divine disapproval on top of everyone else's when we fail. Struggles with sin and brokenness are inefficient, they slow down the system, they hinder institutional expansion and the triumphant image Church, Inc. relies on to attract more members. Therefore, "problem people" must be contained or made invisible until such time as their testimony of transformation is sufficiently inspiring to be mined for useful content. When a problem person has the title "pastor," the banishment is often swift and permanent, as Bill discovered.

His story of ministry pressure and addiction is more common that we'd like to admit, and even those who see the problem are reluctant to assign responsibility beyond the church leader's own failure to get help. Addiction is usually attributed to individual vice or family history rather than systemic ministry failures. Even Bill was of this mindset. He placed no blame on anyone but himself; he was not claiming to be a victim. In our culture of shifting blame, his willingness to take personal responsibility was admirable, but what if there's more to the story? What if the way we structure ministry is part of the problem? Bill's experience in the church hadn't helped him overcome alcoholism, but had it actually made the problem worse?

That's the question Sally Morgenthaler asked after her husband's addiction resulted in a felony conviction and eight years in prison. He was a youth pastor. "Just because we put a 'ministry' tag on certain church leadership norms doesn't make them good," Morgenthaler wrote years later. She concluded that some ministry realities "are toxic, undermining emotional and spiritual health. . . . [The] way ministry is set up, idealized, and practiced may actually fuel addictive behavior."[2] Morganthaler had discovered the dark side of Church, Inc. In no way did Morganthaler excuse her husband's criminal behavior or blame the church for his addiction; instead she explained how popular ministry structures create an iniquity incubator in which a pastor's personal insecurities and temptations can grow to catastrophic proportions.

As I sat silently listening to Bill's story, I felt powerless. I was out of my depth. I had no theological category or guidelines for engaging someone like Bill. I had been taught how to talk to the terminally ill. I had books of strategies for growing churches and structuring discipleship programs. I had passages of Scripture marked in my Bible for grieving families, and I even had guidelines for how to survey a community when launching a new church program. But seminary had not prepared me with a three-point process for ministering to a dejected alcoholic pastor. I suspected none existed.

This realization triggered a sudden realization: I was part of the problem. I was being trained to lead within Church, Inc., but it was Church, Inc. that had, in part, put Bill in the hospital bed. Could the very thing I had been sold as the remedy to the world's problems actually be part of its disease?

When Bill finally finished talking, it felt like it was my turn to speak, to offer advice, to minister. I stayed silent. I could feel myself shrinking even more within my borrowed chaplain suit. Looking for an escape from the room and the awkwardness, I spoke timidly.

"Thank you for sharing so honestly," I said. "I appreciate your advice."

Bill looked away as I rose and moved for the door. Like everyone else in Bill's life, I knew I'd be more comfortable once I didn't have to look at him anymore, once he was invisible again and my illusion of Church, Inc. was restored. It wasn't until I grabbed the door handle to exit that I remembered my calling. "In this room you represent the presence of God." I was not there to represent the chaplaincy office of the hospital. I was not there to represent

Church, Inc. I was not there to represent a young seminary student named Skye. I was there to incarnate the presence of God, if only for a few minutes, to an utterly broken man who had lost his dignity.

I looked back at Bill and was reminded of Peter's encounter with the lame beggar at the Beautiful Gate. "I have no silver and gold," the apostle said, "but what I do have I give to you" (Acts 3:6). I had no advice or wisdom for Bill, but I did have the presence of Jesus. I could give him that. I returned to my chair by his bed.

"Bill, I don't know how to help you," I said, "but I'd like to stay here if that's okay." He took my hand tightly in his and began to weep. So did I. I don't know how long we cried, but our weeping was a liturgy without words. The tears were a silent sacrament containing confession and absolution, condemnation and compassion, burial and resurrection. I knew Bill wasn't clinging to me—he was clinging to God, just as I wasn't merely crying over Bill's sin—I was mourning my own. The moment was utterly human and yet mysteriously divine. It was ministry.

Our calling as pastors is to rehabilitate, to give people back the dignity the world has taken away. That happens when we carry the presence of God into every room we enter and into every life we encounter, and there announce the good news that they are created in the image of God and are inherently worthy of love, and that God has revealed the extent of His love for them through Jesus' life, death, resurrection, and ascension. This work of restoring dignity is always incarnate; it cannot be accomplished merely through systems, structures, or programs. Rehabilitation requires the present and mysterious mingling of humanity and divinity.

To be a pastor is to represent the presence of God, who is present with others. It is to see people—full, embodied, messy, sinful, beautiful people—and to see them the way Jesus does, as creatures of unsurpassable worth. To be a pastor is to freely give what we possess, which is nothing the world values and yet is the most valuable thing in all the world. The world values what is useful, which is what Church, Inc. tries to provide, but all we have is Jesus. To be a pastor is to say, "I have no silver and gold, but what I do have I give to you."

NOTES

Dedication

1. Gen. 6:4 (King James Version).

Introduction

1. Richard Halverson, from a speech before the General Assembly of the Presbyterian Church, 1984, quoted by Barry Popik, "Entry from March 25, 2014: 'When Christianity came to America, it became a business,'" *BarryPopik.com*, March 25, 2014, http://www.barrypopik.com/index .php/new_york_city/entry/when_christianity_came_to_america_it_ became_a_business.

Chapter 3: Wastefulness

1. Andy Crouch, "The Gospel: How is Art a Gift, a Calling, and an Obedience?" in *For the Beauty of the Church: Casting a Vision for the Arts*, edited by David O. Taylor (Grand Rapids: Baker Books, 2010), 40.

Chapter 4: Vampires

1. Anne Rice, quoted in "Jesus: The Ultimate Supernatural Hero," Beliefnet. com, http://www.beliefnet.com/faiths/christianity/2005/11/jesus-the-ultimate-supernatural-hero.aspx?.

2. Josh Packard and Ashleigh Hope, *Church Refugees* (Loveland, CO: Group Publishing, 2015).

3. Lydia Saad, "Confidence in Religion at New Low, but Not Among Catholics," *Gallup*, June 17, 2015, http://www.gallup.com/poll/183674/confidence-religion-new-low-not-among-catholics.aspx.

4. Jim Norman, "Americans' Confidence in Institutions Stays Low," *Gallup*, June 13, 2016, http://www.gallup.com/poll/192581/americans-confidence-institutions-stays-low.aspx.

5. Ron Fournier and Sophie Quinton, "How Americans Lost Trust in Our Greatest Institutions," *The Atlantic*, April 20, 2012, https://www.theatlantic.com/politics/archive/2012/04/how-americans-lost-trust-in-our-greatest-institutions/256163/.

6. "Infographic: Millennial Entrepreneurship Ascending," *rasmussen.edu*, September 23, 2013, http://www.rasmussen.edu/student-life/blogs/main/infographic-millenial-entrepreneurship/.

Chapter 6: Dramas

1. Thomas R. Kelly, *A Testament of Devotion* (New York: HarperCollins, 1992), 25.

Chapter 7: Enemies

1. "Your Church's Priorities?" *Leadership Journal*, Spring 2005, http://www.christianitytoday.com/pastors/2005/spring/2.7.html.

Chapter 8: Simplicity

1. Ben Leubsdorf, "Decline in Church-Building Reflects Changed Tastes and Times," *The Wall Street Journal*, Dec. 4, 2014, https://www.wsj.com/articles/decline-in-church-building-reflects-changed-tastes-and-times-1417714642.

Chapter 9: Complexity

1. Frank Zappa, *The Real Frank Zappa* (New York: Poseidon Press, 1989), 203.

2. Kevin McSpadden, "You Now Have a Shorter Attention Span Than a Goldfish," *Time*, May 14, 2015, http://time.com/3858309/attention-spans-goldfish/.

3. Jim Norman, "Americans' Confidence in Institutions Stays Low," *Gallup*, June 13, 2016, http://www.gallup.com/poll/192581/americans-confidence-institutions-stays-low.aspx.

Chapter 10: Redundancy

1. James Ball, "How Safe Is Air Travel Really?" *The Guardian*, July 24, 2014, https://www.theguardian.com/commentisfree/2014/jul/24/avoid-air-travel-mh17-math-risk-guide.

2. Nassim Nicholas Taleb, *Antifragile: Things That Gain from Disorder* (New York: Random House, 2014).

3. "Next & Level," *Leadership Journal*, Spring 2008, http://www.christianitytoday.com/pastors/2008/spring/3.24.html.

Chapter 12: Illumination

1. Silvia Donati, "Mosaic Wonder: The Mausoleum of Galla Placidia in Ravenna," *Italy Magazine*, May 19, 2016, http://www.italymagazine.com/news/mosaic-wonder-mausoleum-galla-placidia-ravenna.

2. Tatyana Tolstaya, "See the Other Side," *The New Yorker*, March 12, 2007, http://www.newyorker.com/magazine/2007/03/12/see-the-other-side.

3. Ibid.

4. Doug Pagitt, *Preaching Re-Imagined: The Role of the Sermon in Communities of Faith* (Grand Rapids: Zondervan, 2005).

5. Dallas Willard, "Rethinking Evangelism," dwillard.org, http://www.dwillard.org/articles/artview.asp?artID=53.

Chapter 13: Comfort

1. Kells Hetherington, "Automation in the air dulls pilot skill," *Daily Caller*, August 30, 2011, http://dailycaller.com/2011/08/30/automation-in-the-air-dulls-pilot-skill/.

2. Jag Bhalla, "Kahneman's Mind-Clarifying Strangers: System 1 & System 2," *Big Think*, http://bigthink.com/errors-we-live-by/kahnemans-mind-clarifying-biases.

Chapter 14: Rest

1. Dean Schabner, "Americans: Overworked, Overstressed," ABC News, http://abcnews.go.com/US/story?id=93604&page=1.

2. "Three Trends on Faith, Work, and Calling," Barna Group, February 11, 2014, https://www.barna.com/research/three-trends-on-faith-work-and-calling/.

3. Fox Van Allen, "Survey: Almost All Smartphone Owners Do the Same Thing When They Wake Up," *TIME*, October 15, 2013, http://techland.time.com/2013/10/15/survey-almost-all-smartphone-owners-do-the-same-thing-when-they-wake-up/.

4. "The Myth of Multitasking," *Talk of the Nation*, National Public Radio, May 10, 2013, http://www.npr.org/2013/05/10/182861382 the-myth-of-multitasking.

5. Henri Nouwen, "From Solitude to Community to Ministry," *Leadership Journal*, Spring 1995, http://www.christianitytoday.com/pastors/1995/spring/5l280.html.

6. Paul Vitello, "William Pogue, Astronaut Who Staged a Strike in Space, Dies at 84," *The New York Times*, March 10, 2014, https://www.nytimes.com/2014/03/11/science/space/william-r-pogue-astronaut-who-flew-longest-skylab-mission-is-dead-at-84.html.

Chapter 18: Consumers

1. Jeanne Willette, "Jean Baudrillard and the System of Objects," *Art History Unstuffed*, September 5, 2014, http://arthistoryunstuffed.com/jean-baudrillard-system-of-objects/

2. Po Bronson, "How We Spend Our Leisure Time," *Time*, Oct. 23, 2006, http://content.time.com/time/nation/article/0,8599,1549394,00.html.

3. Pete Ward, *Liquid Church* (Grand Rapids: Baker Publishing Group, 2001), 60.

4. Mark Riddle, "Rant #2—The Christian Bookstore," *TheOoze.com*, April 11, 2002, https://web.archive.org/web/20020808062134/http://www.theooze.com:80/articles/read.cfm?ID=407&CATID=4.

5. From an 1897 article in *Harper's Weekly*, cited in *Major Problems in American Popular Culture*, edited by Kathleen Franz and Susan Smulyan (Boston: Wadsworth, Cengage Learning, 2012), 183.

6. Rodney Clapp, "Why the Devil Takes VISA," *Christianity Today*, October 7, 1996, http://www.christianitytoday.com/ct/1996/october7/6tb018.html.

7. Victor Lebow, quoted by Alan Thein Durning in *How Much Is Enough?* (New York: W. W. Norton & Co., 1992), 21.

8. Roger Finke and Rodney Stark, *The Churching of America, 1776–2005* (New Brunswick, NJ: Rutgers University Press, 2006), 9.

9. Rebecca Barnes, "Changing up church: Multi-venue churches, Part 1," *Church Central*, June 3, 2004, https://www.churchcentral.com/news/changing-up-church-multi-venue-churches-part-1/

10. George Barna, *Revolution* (Carol Stream, IL: Tyndale House Publishing, 2005), 66.

11. Tony Jones, "Youth and Religion: An Interview with Christian Smith," *Youth Specialties*, October 2, 2009, http://youthspecialties.com/blog/youth-and-religion-an-interview-with-christian-smith/.

Chapter 19: Witness

1. Thomas Kelly, *A Testament of Devotion* (San Francisco: HarperSanFrancisco, 1941), 9.

Chapter 21: Justice

1. John Stott, *Christian Mission in the Modern World* (Downers Grove, IL: InterVarsity Press, 1975), 41.

2. Ibid., 47–48.

Chapter 22: Missionalism

1. Gordon MacDonald, "Dangers of Missionalism," *Leadership Journal*, Winter 2007, http://www.christianitytoday.com/pastors/2007/winter/16.38.html.

2. Phil Vischer, *Me, Myself, and Bob* (Nashville: Thomas Nelson, 2007), 238.

Chapter 24: Rehabilitation

1. *Birdman of Alcatraz*, directed by John Frankenheimer (1962).

2. Sally Morgenthaler, "Does Ministry Fuel Addictive Behavior?" *Leadership Journal*, Winter 2006, http://www.christianitytoday.com/pastors/2006/winter/24.58.html.

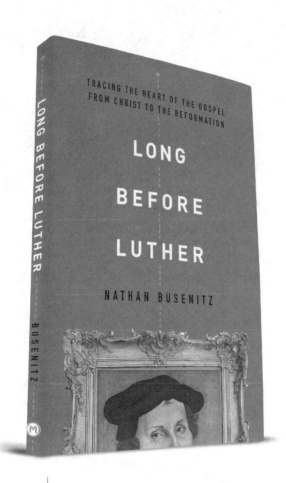

DOES THE WORLD MAKE YOU DIZZY?

A Lot Is Expected of a Pastor, But What Is ESSENTIAL?

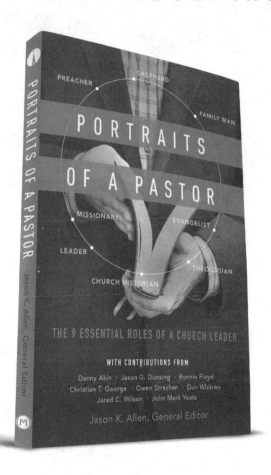